CRYPTOCURRENCY FOR BEGINNERS

STEP-BY-STEP GUIDE TO CRYPTO TRADING, WALLET SECURITY & BLOCKCHAIN BASICS TO AVOID COMMON SCAMS, PROTECT INVESTMENTS, AND UNDERSTAND LEGAL & TAX IMPLICATIONS

PF TAYLOR

CONTENTS

Introduction 5

1. UNDERSTANDING CRYPTOCURRENCY FUNDAMENTALS 7
1.1 What is Cryptocurrency? 8
1.2 Cryptocurrency: Advantages vs. Disadvantages 9
1.3 Blockchain Technology: The Backbone of Crypto 11
1.4 Demystifying Cryptocurrency Jargon 15
1.5 Bitcoin and Beyond: Exploring Major Cryptocurrencies 16
1.6 Crypto Quiz: Test Your Knowledge 21

2. CHOOSING AND SECURING YOUR WALLET 24
2.1 Step-by-Step Wallet Setup for Beginners 26
2.2 Securing Your Digital Wallet Against Threats 28
2.3 Troubleshooting Common Wallet Issues 30
2.4 Wallet Quiz: Test Your Knowledge 32

3. NAVIGATING CRYPTOCURRENCY EXCHANGES 35
3.1 The Importance of KYC and Verification Processes 37
3.2 Comparing Exchange Features and Fees 38
3.3 Avoiding Exchange Scams: Red Flags to Watch For 40
3.4 Exchange Quiz: Test Your Knowledge 42

4. DEVELOPING A PERSONALIZED TRADING PLAN 45
4.1 Identifying Your Risk Tolerance 47
4.2 Selecting Trading Strategies: Day, Swing, and Long-Term 49
4.3 Implementing Your Plan: Start Small and Begin with Paper Trading 51
4.4 Trading Plan Checklist 52

5. BUILDING A CRYPTOCURRENCY PORTFOLIO 54
5.1 Risk Assessment: Balancing High and Low Volatility Assets 56
5.2 Long-Term vs. Short-Term Investments: Pros and Cons 57
5.3 Real-Life Case Studies: Successful Portfolio Examples 59
5.4 Cryptocurrency Portfolio Considerations 60

6. MASTERING MARKET ANALYSIS 64
6.1 Technical Analysis: Charts, Patterns, and Technical Indicators 65
6.2 Fundamental Analysis: Economic and Financial Factors 74
6.3 Applying Analysis in Real-Life Scenarios 76

7. EFFECTIVE RISK MANAGEMENT 79
7.1 Diversification Strategies to Minimize Risk 80
7.2 Strategies to Avoid Emotional Trading Decisions 82
7.3 Learning from Losses: Turning Mistakes into Lessons 83
7.4 Risk Management Quiz: Test Your Knowledge 85

8. ENTRY AND EXIT STRATEGIES 88
8.1 Setting Profitable Exit Strategies 91
8.2 Timing the Market: Myths vs. Reality 93
8.3 Adapting Strategies to Market Changes 94
8.4 Entry and Exit Quiz: Test Your Knowledge 96

9. SECURITY AND SCAM PREVENTION 99
9.1 Identifying Common Cryptocurrency Scams 99
9.2 Scam Prevention Steps 101
9.3 Strengthening Security Measures for Digital Assets 101
9.4 Personal Security Enhancement Guide 103
9.5 Real-Life Scam Examples and How to Avoid Them 103

10. STAYING INFORMED AND CONNECTED 107
10.1 Joining Cryptocurrency Communities for Support 109
10.2 Tools for Monitoring Your Investments 110
10.3 Continuous Learning: Recommended Resources 112

11. NAVIGATING LEGAL AND TAX CONSIDERATIONS 115
11.1 Tax Implications of Crypto: What You Need to Know 117
11.2 Tracking Transactions for Tax Purposes 119
11.3 Legal and Tax Resources 120
11.4 New U.S. Crypto Tax Rules 122
11.5 Real-Life Tax Scenarios: Lessons Learned 122
11.6 Regulatory and Tax Resources 124

Conclusion 129
References 131

INTRODUCTION

In the last decade, a financial revolution has been quietly unfolding, challenging the very foundations of our global economy. This revolution is cryptocurrency – a digital form of money transforming how we think about value, ownership, and trust. Since the creation of Bitcoin in 2009, the total market capitalization of cryptocurrencies has grown from zero to over $1 trillion, attracting millions of investors worldwide.

As a finance professional with years of experience in accounting and risk assessment, I found myself drawn to the potential of this emerging asset class. Like many of you, I was initially skeptical and overwhelmed by the technical jargon and complexity surrounding cryptocurrency. But as I delved deeper, I realized that beneath the surface lay a powerful technology with the potential to reshape our financial future.

This book, "Cryptocurrency for Beginners," is the result of my journey into the world of digital assets. It's a comprehensive guide designed to simplify the basics of cryptocurrency, providing you with the tools and knowledge you need to navigate this exciting but often confusing landscape. Whether you're a complete novice or have some experience with investing, this book will help you understand the fundamentals of trading, wallet security, and market dynamics.

INTRODUCTION

The world of cryptocurrency is rapidly evolving, with new projects, technologies, and regulations emerging daily. It can be both exhilarating and daunting, filled with stories of overnight millionaires and costly scams. That's why I've made it my mission to create a resource that cuts through the noise and provides clear, actionable insights for beginners.

Throughout this book, we'll cover everything from setting up your first wallet to analyzing market trends and managing risk. You'll learn how to research and evaluate different cryptocurrencies, understand the impact of news events on prices, and develop a trading plan that aligns with your goals and risk tolerance. We'll also explore the legal and tax implications of investing in cryptocurrency, ensuring that you stay compliant and informed.

Inside this book, you'll find step-by-step guides, interactive quizzes, and insights from experienced traders and industry experts. By the end of this book, you'll have the skills and confidence to make informed investment decisions and participate in the exciting world of cryptocurrency.

But this book is more than just a guide to investing. It's also an invitation to join a growing community of individuals who are passionate about the potential of blockchain technology and decentralized finance. As you learn and grow, you'll discover new opportunities to connect with like-minded people, contribute to innovative projects, and shape the future of money.

So whether you're dreaming of financial freedom, curious about the technology behind Bitcoin, or simply looking to diversify your investment portfolio, this book is your gateway to the world of cryptocurrency. Let's dive in together and unlock the power of digital assets to transform your financial future.

CHAPTER 1
UNDERSTANDING CRYPTOCURRENCY FUNDAMENTALS

ON MAY 22, 2010, a man named Laszlo Hanyecz made what is now considered one of the most famous transactions in the history of cryptocurrency and is now known as Bitcoin Pizza Day. He bought two pizzas for 10,000 Bitcoin, which was worth $41 then but would be worth hundreds of millions of dollars today. At the time, this transaction seemed trivial, but it marked the beginning of using digital currency in the real world. It was a pivotal moment that highlighted both the potential and the unpredictability of cryptocurrencies. This chapter aims to unpack the basics of cryptocurrency and why it's reshaping how we think about money.

1.1 WHAT IS CRYPTOCURRENCY?

Cryptocurrency is essentially digital cash. Unlike traditional money, it doesn't rely on banks or governments to verify transactions. Instead, it operates on a technology called blockchain, which is a decentralized ledger of all transactions that take place across a network of computers. This means that when you send or receive cryptocurrency, it's done directly between you and the other party, with no middleman involved. This peer-to-peer nature is one of the most intriguing aspects of cryptocurrency because it allows for transactions to occur almost instantly and at a lower cost than traditional financial systems.

What makes cryptocurrencies stand out from traditional fiat currencies is their decentralized nature. They aren't controlled by a central authority like a government or a bank. This decentralization is powered by cryptographic technology, which not only secures transactions but also ensures that cryptocurrencies are extremely difficult to counterfeit. Unlike traditional currencies, where you might incur hefty fees for cross-border transactions, cryptocurrencies offer a global reach without the need for currency exchange. However, it's important to note that the value of cryptocurrencies can fluctuate wildly due to market factors and investor sentiment, which can be both exciting and challenging for new investors.

The journey of cryptocurrencies began with the birth of Bitcoin in 2009, created by the mysterious figure known as Satoshi Nakamoto. This marked the start of a new era in digital finance. Bitcoin's success paved the way for many other cryptocurrencies, known as altcoins, each with unique features and purposes. Over the years, technological advancements have spurred the development of these digital assets, each contributing to the rich tapestry that is the cryptocurrency landscape today.

1.2 CRYPTOCURRENCY: ADVANTAGES VS. DISADVANTAGES

Cryptocurrency is transforming the financial landscape, offering groundbreaking opportunities and significant challenges. This section explores both the advantages and disadvantages of digital currencies. Understanding the pros and cons is crucial for anyone looking to navigate the complex world of digital assets. Whether you're considering cryptocurrency for transactions, investment, or innovation, this balanced perspective will equip you with the knowledge needed to approach this dynamic market with confidence.

Advantages of Cryptocurrency

Decentralization

- Removes the need for banks or intermediaries
- Enables peer-to-peer transactions without third parties
- Reduces transaction costs and processing delays

Security & Transparency

- Blockchain technology ensures every transaction is recorded on a public ledger
- Data cannot be altered without network consensus, reducing fraud risk
- Minimizes identity theft and enhances financial security

Financial Inclusion

- Provides access to financial services for the unbanked and underbanked
- Requires only an internet connection and a digital wallet

Faster & Cheaper Transactions

- Eliminates bank processing delays
- Makes cross-border payments more affordable and efficient

Investment Opportunities

- Potential for high returns due to market growth and innovation
- Serves as a hedge against inflation
- Allows for portfolio diversification

Disadvantages of Cryptocurrency

Market Volatility

- Highly unpredictable price fluctuations
- Can gain or lose double-digit percentages within hours

Security Risks

- Hacking, phishing scams, and theft are common threats
- Irreversible transactions – lost funds cannot be recovered
- Requires strong security measures to protect assets

Regulatory Uncertainty

- Governments are still developing cryptocurrency laws
- Potential for new taxes or restrictions
- Legal landscape varies by region

Lack of Consumer Protection

- No fraud protection like traditional banks
- Transactions are final, making it risky for mistakes or scams

Technical Complexity

- Managing private keys and securing wallets requires knowledge
- Blockchain mechanics can be complicated for beginners
- Risk of user errors leading to lost funds

High-Risk, High-Reward Investment

- Requires careful consideration before investing
- Demands ongoing education and security awareness

While cryptocurrency presents exciting opportunities, it also comes with risks that require careful consideration. As you navigate this evolving space, balancing these advantages and disadvantages is key to making sound investment decisions.

1.3 BLOCKCHAIN TECHNOLOGY: THE BACKBONE OF CRYPTO

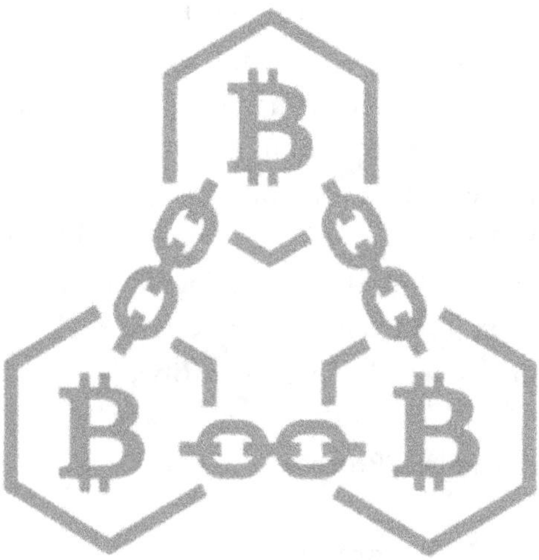

Blockchain technology is like a digital notebook that everyone can see but no one can erase or change once something is written in it. Imagine a group of friends keeping a shared record of transactions. Every time someone makes a transaction, they write it down in a book, and everyone gets a copy. Once the page is full, it gets locked, and a new page starts. But before locking the page, everyone checks and agrees that all transactions are correct.

In technical terms, each page is called a "block," and these blocks are linked together in a chain, forming a secure and unchangeable history of transactions – hence the name "blockchain." Since every participant in the network has a copy, no single person or organization can alter past records, making blockchain very secure.

To preserve the integrity of each block, blockchain networks use a cryptographic hash of all the transactions within the block along with a reference to the previous block. A hash is like a digital fingerprint made from data. It is the output of a cryptographic hash function that converts any data into a fixed-length string of letters and numbers. Each block contains a list of all transactions in the block, a block header, and a block number. The block header contains information on the current block as well as the hash of the previous block's header, creating a chain of blocks. This linking of blocks through their hashes ensures that once a block is added to the chain, modifying it would require recalculating that block and every subsequent block and getting a majority of the network's miners to accept the new version of the blockchain. This would require an immense amount of computational power and would be prohibitively expensive. Since changing a block in the blockchain would require overwhelming resources and coordination, it would be extremely difficult and practically infeasible. In addition, any attempt to change block data can be easily detected by network participants, which creates security and trust in the system.

Step-by-Step Blockchain Process:

- **Transaction Initiation**
  - A person sends digital assets (like cryptocurrency) to another person.

- **Transaction Verification**
    - Computers (nodes) in the blockchain network check if the transaction is valid using cryptographic rules.
    - This verification ensures the sender has enough funds and isn't trying to spend the same asset twice (prevents fraud).

- **Block Creation**
    - Approved transactions are grouped together to form a **block**. Each block contains:
        - A list of transactions
        - A timestamp
        - A reference (hash) to the previous block.

- **Consensus Mechanism (Validation Process)**
    - To ensure security and agreement, the network must decide which block to add next. This is done through **consensus mechanisms**, such as:
        - **Proof of Work (PoW)** – Miners compete to solve complex mathematical puzzles. The first to solve it gets to add the block (used in Bitcoin).
        - **Proof of Stake (PoS)** – Validators are chosen based on the amount of cryptocurrency they hold and are willing to "stake" as collateral (used in Ethereum 2.0).

- **Adding the Block to the Chain**
    - Once verified, the new block is added to the blockchain and linked to the previous block, forming a continuous chain.
    - Each block contains a unique code **(hash)** that connects it to the previous block, ensuring security.

- **Transaction Completion**
    - The transaction is recorded permanently, and all network participants get an updated copy of the blockchain.

- No one can alter or delete past transactions, ensuring transparency and security.

Types of Blockchains

Blockchain technology comes in different forms, each with its own use case. Public blockchains, like Bitcoin and Ethereum, allow anyone to access and view transactions, making them decentralized and open. Private blockchains restrict access to authorized users, offering more control and privacy. Consortium blockchains sit in the middle, where a group of organizations governs the network, providing a balance between decentralization and control. Each type of blockchain serves a specific purpose, catering to the needs of different industries and applications.

Despite its advantages, blockchain does face some challenges. Scalability is a significant issue, as processing a large number of transactions can slow down the network. This has been a topic of ongoing research and development, with various solutions being explored. Energy consumption is another concern, particularly with Proof of Work systems, where mining requires substantial computing power. This has led to environmental debates and the search for more efficient consensus mechanisms, such as Proof of Stake.

Beyond cryptocurrency, blockchain technology is making waves across various industries. In supply chain management, it provides a transparent and tamper-proof record of product movement, enhancing efficiency and reducing fraud. Healthcare is also benefiting, with blockchain enabling secure sharing of patient records, improving privacy and data integrity. Digital identity verification is another area where blockchain shines, offering a secure and reliable way to verify identities without the need for intermediaries. Smart contracts, self-executing contracts with predefined rules, are transforming industries by automating and enforcing agreements without human intervention, reducing costs and enhancing trust. Given blockchain's advantages – such as enhanced traceability, transparency, efficiency, and security – its adoption is expected to keep growing across various industries.

1.4 DEMYSTIFYING CRYPTOCURRENCY JARGON

Cryptocurrency can feel like a foreign language, filled with terms and phrases that seem puzzling at first glance. But once you break it down, it's easier to grasp. In the fast-paced world of cryptocurrency, knowledge is power. Learning the lingo empowers you to stay ahead, make informed choices, and avoid common pitfalls. Whether you're reading investment articles, participating in discussions, or simply exploring the crypto space, a solid grasp of this jargon will enhance your understanding and decision-making ability, opening doors to new opportunities and a deeper appreciation of the crypto world.

Key Terms & Definitions

- **Bitcoin (BTC)** – The first and most well-known cryptocurrency, often called "digital gold."
- **Altcoins** – Any cryptocurrency other than Bitcoin, with various features and use cases (e.g., Ethereum, Litecoin, Cardano).
- **NFTs (Non-Fungible Tokens)** – Unique digital assets representing ownership of digital art, music, or collectibles, similar to a one-of-a-kind baseball card.
- **Fiat Currency** – Traditional currency, like US Dollar or Euro, issued by governments.
- **Blockchain** – A decentralized digital ledger that records transactions across many computers securely.
- **Mining** – The process by which new cryptocurrency coins are created, using computer power to solve complex mathematical programs and validate transactions on the blockchain.
- **Wallet** – A digital tool to store and manage your cryptocurrencies, available as software (online) or hardware (offline).
- **Exchange** - A platform where cryptocurrencies can be bought, sold, or traded.

- **HODL** – A slang term meaning "Hold on for Dear Life" used to describe keeping cryptocurrency long-term rather than selling it.
- **ICO (Initial Coin Offering)** – A fundraising method where new cryptocurrencies sell tokens to early investors.
- **Bull Market** – A period of rising prices in the market, leading to widespread optimism and investment.
- **Bear Market** – A period of declining prices, causing pessimism and potential sell-off among investors.
- **Pump and Dump** – A scheme where an asset's price is artificially inflated before insiders sell off their holdings, leading to a price crash.
- **Whale** – An individual or organization holding large amounts of a cryptocurrency, capable of influencing the market due to the size of their holdings.
- **Smart Contract** – Self-executing contract with the terms of the agreement directly written into code, running on blockchain platforms.

1.5 BITCOIN AND BEYOND: EXPLORING MAJOR CRYPTOCURRENCIES

Bitcoin (BTC) is the pioneer in digital currencies, the brainchild of an enigmatic figure known as Satoshi Nakamoto. In 2008, Nakamoto released a whitepaper that laid the groundwork for Bitcoin as a decentralized digital currency, operating without a central authority, such as a government or bank. This innovation is frequently described as the digital equivalent of gold because of its rarity and value preservation. Unlike traditional currencies with unlimited supply, Bitcoin has a fixed supply and is permanently capped at 21 million coins. This limit is primarily to prevent inflation and create scarcity, making Bitcoin similar to a precious resource like gold, which is valuable partly because it is rare. By having a fixed maximum supply, Bitcoin aims to maintain its value and avoid the pitfalls of currencies controlled by governments and central banks, which can print money endlessly. This scarcity encourages people to view Bitcoin as a valuable asset, promoting its adoption and investment as a digital form of money.

Bitcoins are created through the mining process. **Mining** is like a race where miners use powerful computers to solve complex mathematical puzzles. The first miner to solve the puzzle for the block is allowed to add that block to the blockchain and receives a mining reward. Initially, the reward was 50 bitcoins per block. The mining reward is reduced every four years by halving. Currently, the reward is 3.125 bitcoins per block, and based on the chart below will be .10 in 2044. Since new bitcoins are created through mining, the number of coins created will also be halved every year, with only 41,016 bitcoins/year being created after the halving in 2044. The last Bitcoin is expected to be created around 2140.

Bitcoin's impact on the financial world has been monumental, challenging traditional banking and payment systems and providing an alternative store of value. As an investment, Bitcoin offers potential rewards, but it also comes with challenges, including significant price volatility and regulatory scrutiny. Investors must weigh these factors when considering Bitcoin as part of their portfolios.

Ethereum (ETH) entered the scene as a formidable challenger, introducing the revolutionary concept of smart contracts. Unlike Bitcoin, which is primarily a digital currency, Ethereum is a platform that allows developers to build decentralized applications, or dApps, on its blockchain. At the heart of Ethereum is the Ethereum Virtual Machine (EVM), which executes these programmable contracts autonomously, effectively replacing intermediaries. This has unlocked a myriad of possibilities across various sectors. For example, decentralized finance (DeFi) platforms have emerged, offering financial services without the need for traditional banks. Ethereum has also facilitated the rise of non-fungible tokens (NFTs), allowing digital art and collectibles to be bought and sold with verifiable ownership. Additionally, decentralized autonomous organizations (DAOs) have taken shape, enabling governance and decision-making processes to occur democratically and transparently on the blockchain.

NFTs (Non-fungible tokens) are unique digital assets stored on a blockchain that certify ownership, authenticity, and scarcity of digital items such as art, collectibles, music, videos, and virtual real estate. Unlike cryptocurrencies like Bitcoin, which are interchangeable, each NFT is distinct and cannot be replicated. NFTs are mainly used for digital art, allowing artists to sell their work directly and earn royalties on resales. They are also popular in gaming, where players can own and trade in-game items, and in the metaverse, where virtual land and assets are bought and sold. Additionally, NFTs serve as collectibles, granting exclusive access to events, memberships, and special perks in online communities. Their value comes from rarity, demand, and utility, making them a blend of digital ownership, investment, and creativity.

Beyond Bitcoin and Ethereum, the world of **altcoins** offers a diverse range of options, each with its own unique attributes.

- Litecoin, for instance, is often dubbed the silver to Bitcoin's gold due to its faster transaction times and lower fees.
- XRP is used for cross-border payments and is gaining traction with financial institutions seeking efficient international transfers.
- Cardano takes a scientific approach, emphasizing peer-reviewed research and a layered architecture for enhanced security and scalability.
- Solana, known for its high-speed transactions, is making waves with its ability to process thousands of transactions per second, appealing to developers looking for efficient platforms.
- Polkadot enables cross-chain interoperability, enabling different blockchains to communicate and share information seamlessly, fostering innovation across networks.

Investing in altcoins presents opportunities for higher returns compared to more established cryptocurrencies like Bitcoin and

Ethereum, especially as they venture into specialized niches such as privacy coins and DeFi. However, these potential rewards come with inherent risks. Altcoins often face greater market volatility and liquidity concerns, making it challenging to predict their price movements. Regulatory risks also loom as governments worldwide grapple with how to classify and oversee these digital assets.

For those interested in exploring altcoin investments, it's vital to assess the fundamentals of each project, scrutinize the credibility of the development team, and understand the project's goals. Active community engagement and ongoing developments can also offer valuable insights into the potential success of an altcoin.

Stablecoins, such as Tether (USDT) and USD Coin (USDC), are a type of cryptocurrency designed to maintain a stable value relative to a specific asset, typically a fiat currency like the US Dollar, or other assets like precious metals. Their value remains relatively stable and can provide a safe haven during market volatility. Some investors will quickly move their funds into stablecoins to preserve value during times of market turbulence.

When comparing and contrasting cryptocurrencies, several factors come into play. Consensus mechanisms, for instance, vary across platforms, influencing their security and scalability. Bitcoin relies on Proof of Work, demanding significant computational power, while newer networks like Cardano use Proof of Stake, which is more energy-efficient. The use cases and market positioning of each cryptocurrency also differ. Bitcoin is often viewed as a store of value, akin to digital gold, while Ethereum is recognized for its versatility in enabling smart contracts and dApps. Altcoins cater to specific needs, such as cross-border payments and interoperability; and stablecoins serve as a hedge against volatility. Understanding these nuances is crucial for making informed decisions in the dynamic and ever-evolving cryptocurrency landscape.

1.6 CRYPTO QUIZ: TEST YOUR KNOWLEDGE

You've now taken in a wealth of information about cryptocurrency and blockchain. It's a lot to digest, and it's perfectly normal to feel overwhelmed. But don't worry, that's why this section is here. By testing your understanding, you can reinforce what you've learned and identify areas that need more focus. Consider it your personal checkpoint to gauge how comfortable you are with these new concepts.

True or False

1. Blockchain technology ensures that once a transaction is recorded, it cannot be changed. (True/False)
2. All cryptocurrencies are mined in the same way as Bitcoin. (True/False)

Multiple Choice

3. Which of the following best describes a blockchain?
   - A) A centralized database managed by a single organization
   - B) A distributed ledger maintained by a network of computers
   - C) A type of cryptocurrency used for transactions
4. What was the primary purpose of Bitcoin when it was first introduced?
   - A) To be a stable digital currency
   - B) To enable peer-to-peer transactions without a central authority
   - C) To replace all forms of fiat currency immediately
5. What is a common challenge associated with cryptocurrencies?
   - A) High transaction fees similar to banks
   - B) Lack of security in blockchain technology
   - C) Market volatility
6. Which of the following accurately describes an altcoin?

- A) The first digital currency ever created
- B) Any digital currency other than Bitcoin
- C) A digital currency controlled by a central bank

Answers & Explanations

1. True
   - *Explanation:* The immutability of records is one of the core security features of blockchain.
2. False
   - *Explanation:* While Bitcoin uses mining, other cryptocurrencies may use different methods, such as staking or initial coin offerings (ICOs).
3. B) A distributed ledger maintained by a network of computers
   - *Explanation:* A blockchain is a distributed ledger maintained by a network of computers, ensuring transparency and security.
4. B) To enable peer-to-peer transactions without a central authority
   - *Explanation:* Bitcoin was designed to facilitate peer-to-peer transactions without the need for banks or intermediaries.
5. C) Market volatility
   - *Explanation:* Market volatility is a significant challenge, as cryptocurrency prices can fluctuate rapidly.
6. B) Any digital currency other than Bitcoin
   - *Explanation:* An altcoin is any cryptocurrency other than Bitcoin that offers a wide range of features and uses.

Final Thoughts

Remember, this quiz is a tool to help you solidify your understanding and pinpoint any areas that might need revisiting. The world of cryptocurrency is vast and ever-evolving, and there's always more to learn. As you continue your exploration, keep in mind the opportunities and challenges that come with this innovative technology. The key is to stay curious and open-minded, ready to adapt to new developments and insights.

As you move forward, know that you're not alone in this learning process. Countless individuals are on similar paths, exploring the potential of digital currencies and blockchain technology. By connecting with others and engaging in ongoing education, you can build a strong foundation of knowledge and confidence. Embrace the excitement and possibilities that come with understanding cryptocurrency. Let this be the beginning of a rewarding venture into the digital world.

CHAPTER 2

CHOOSING AND SECURING YOUR WALLET

IMAGINE WALKING into a bank vault filled with gold bars, each representing your hard-earned money, except this vault exists digitally, and you hold the key. This is what a cryptocurrency wallet is like – your personal vault in the vast digital world. Choosing the right wallet is crucial because it determines how securely you can store and access your digital assets. Understanding the different types of wallets is essential as you begin your cryptocurrency journey. Let's dive into the options available and determine which might be the best fit for you.

When it comes to cryptocurrency wallets, you have several options, each with its strengths and weaknesses. First, there are **hardware wallets**, which are sometimes called cold wallets. These are physical devices, similar to USB drives, which store your cryptocurrencies offline. They're incredibly secure because they're not connected to the internet, making them resistant to hacking and cyberattacks. However, they can be less convenient for frequent transactions since you need to connect them to a computer to access your funds. These wallets are often recommended for long-term storage, where security is prioritized over convenience. They come with a cost, as you'll need to purchase the hardware, but the peace of mind they offer can be worth the investment. Today's most popular and widely used hardware wallets are Ledger Nano S, Ledger Nano X, and Trezor.

Next, we have **software wallets**, which are also called hot wallets. You can install these applications on your computer or smartphone or access them through a web browser. They're more accessible than hardware wallets since they allow you to manage your funds from your device. Software wallets balance security and convenience, especially for those who frequently trade or make transactions. They offer features like user-friendly interfaces and integration with exchanges for seamless trading. However, they are more vulnerable to cyber threats since they're connected to the internet. It's essential to keep your device secure and regularly update the wallet software to mitigate these risks. Software wallets are generally free, making them an attractive option for beginners. Today's most popular software wallets are Exodus, Electrum, and Coinomi.

Mobile wallets, like Trust Wallet and Mycelium, bring the convenience of cryptocurrency management to your cell phone. They're perfect for those who want to make transactions on the go. Mobile wallets offer ease of use and portability, much like a digital wallet you carry in your pocket. They're ideal for handling small amounts of cryptocurrency, providing a simple way to send and receive funds. However, the security of mobile wallets depends on the security of your cell phone. Using strong passwords, enabling two-factor authentication, and being cautious about downloading apps from unknown sources is vital to protect your assets.

Choosing the right wallet depends on your specific needs and how you plan to use your cryptocurrencies. If you engage in frequent transactions or need quick access to your funds, a software or mobile wallet might be the best fit. For those looking to store their investment securely for the long haul, hardware wallets offer unparalleled security. Additionally, hybrid solutions are available, combining the benefits of hot and cold storage. Some hardware wallets now come with mobile apps, allowing you to access your funds conveniently while maintaining the security of cold storage.

Trust Wallet and Exodus are good options for beginners. These wallets are known for their ease of use and reliability, making them ideal for newcomers. Trust Wallet offers a simple interface and supports a wide range of cryptocurrencies. Exodus provides excellent customer support and a user-friendly design, with the added advantage of desktop compatibility. Both options provide a solid foundation for managing your digital assets with confidence.

Reflection Section: Determine Your Wallet Type

Reflect on how you plan to use your cryptocurrencies. Are you a frequent trader or a long-term investor? Consider your level of technical expertise and comfort with managing digital security. Write down two or three scenarios where you would use your cryptocurrency and match them with the wallet type that best fits each scenario. This exercise will help you clarify your needs and make an informed decision.

2.1 STEP-BY-STEP WALLET SETUP FOR BEGINNERS

Setting up your first cryptocurrency wallet can feel like assembling a new gadget. At first glance, it might seem daunting, but with a systematic approach, you can get it up and running smoothly. The first step for a software wallet is to download and install the wallet software or app. Ensure you're downloading from the official website or app store to avoid fake versions that could compromise your security. For a hardware wallet, purchase it from a reliable manufacturer, connect it to your computer, and follow the setup instructions. To prevent connectivity issues during setup, it's crucial to ensure that your wallet software is compatible with your device, whether it's a computer or cellphone.

Open the wallet app or connect your hardware wallet to your computer. Most wallets will guide you through the process with prompts. If prompted, select the option to create a new wallet. The wallet will generate a public address (your wallet ID) and a private key (your wallet's security key). Follow the prompts to create your account and set up a strong password. This password will be your first layer of security, so choose one that can't easily be guessed. Don't use your name, date of birth, children's names, etc. Write down the password and keep it in a secure location or save it in a password manager.

Next comes generating and managing your recovery phrase, often called a seed phrase. This series of words serves as a backup to access your wallet and usually includes 12 - 24 words. It's like a master key, and losing it means losing access to your funds. Given its importance, it's crucial to store your recovery phrase securely. Consider methods like writing it down and keeping it in a safe place or using a secure digital backup solution. Avoid storing it on devices connected to the internet to prevent unauthorized access. Don't forget that anyone with access to this phrase can gain control of your wallet.

Configuring security settings and backups is crucial for protecting your digital assets. Many wallets offer two-factor authentication, adding an extra layer of security. Enable this feature to enhance your wallet's protection. Regularly back up your wallet data and keep a copy of your recovery phrase in multiple secure locations.

Visual aids can be beneficial during the setup process. Videos, screenshots, and setup flowcharts can guide you through each step, providing a visual reference that simplifies complex instructions. Many wallet providers offer these resources on their official websites, so take advantage of them. Understanding your wallet's features and settings is key to managing it effectively. Familiarize yourself with the security settings, transaction fees, and limits. Adjust these settings to suit your needs, balancing security with convenience.

The final step is to transfer cryptocurrencies to your wallet. Use QR codes for seamless transfers, eliminating the risk of errors in the transaction address. Before sending any funds, double-check addresses to ensure accuracy. Incorrect addresses can lead to irreversible loss of funds.

Set transaction fees for optimal speed, balancing cost with the urgency of your transaction. Some wallets offer options to prioritize speed over cost, which can be helpful during busy network times. Cryptocurrency transaction fees are influenced by factors like network congestion, transaction size, and the cryptocurrency used. Bitcoin, Ethereum, and other major cryptocurrencies have dynamic fees, which can increase during times of high usage.

To minimize transaction fees:

1. Choose the Right Time – Try to send transactions during times of lower network congestion (e.g., weekends or off-peak hours).
2. Use Layer 2 Solutions – Layer 2 networks, such as Polygon for Ethereum or Lightning Network for Bitcoin, provide faster and cheaper transactions.
3. Adjust your Transaction Fee – Some wallets allow you to manually adjust your transaction fees. Lowering the fee may delay your transaction, but it could save you money on fees.
4. Use Blockchains with Lower Fees – Opt for blockchains with lower transaction fees, such as XRP, Litecoin, or Cardono.

2.2 SECURING YOUR DIGITAL WALLET AGAINST THREATS

Handling your cryptocurrency is like keeping a treasure chest full of valuables; it's crucial to ensure it's protected from prying hands. While securing your wallet may seem complex at first, a thoughtful combination of tools, habits, and awareness can significantly reduce your risk.

1. Strengthen Your Login Security

The first layer of protection starts with your credentials:

- Use **strong, unique passwords** for each crypto-related account. Think of them as the key to your chest – easy for you to remember but nearly impossible for others to guess.
- Avoid reusing passwords across different platforms, as a breach on one could jeopardize others.
- A **password manager** can help you generate and store complex passwords securely.
- Enable **two-factor authentication (2FA)** to add an extra layer of defense. With 2FA, even if someone manages to get your password, they can't access your wallet without a second form of verification, usually a code sent to your phone or email.

2. Stay Alert to Common Threats

Awareness is your first line of defense against the most common digital threats:

- **Phishing scams** often come in the form of emails or fake websites designed to steal your login details. Always verify website URLs for subtle misspellings or odd domains, and avoid clicking on suspicious links.
- **Malware and spyware** can silently infect your devices and harvest sensitive data. Keep your devices secure by regularly **updating software** and using **reputable antivirus programs**.

3. Choose the Right Wallet Type

Your choice of wallet plays a crucial role in overall security:

- **Hardware wallets** and other **cold storage solutions** store your private keys offline, keeping them safe from online attacks. These are ideal for long-term holders or those managing significant amounts of crypto.

- Consider **multi-signature wallets** for an added layer of protection. These require multiple approvals to complete a transaction – like having several keys to unlock your vault.

4. Maintain and Monitor Your Security
Security isn't a one-time task – it's an ongoing process:

- Regularly **update your wallet software** to patch vulnerabilities and protect against emerging threats. Developers frequently release updates to improve security.
- Perform **routine security check-ups**: monitor account activity, audit your setup, and verify that security features are still active and effective.
- **Be Cautious with Online Wallets**: Understand the heightened risks associated with using online wallets, as they are more vulnerable to phishing attacks.
- Stay informed about evolving cybersecurity threats and best practices to remain a step ahead.

5. Schedule Regular Backups

- Frequently update and back up your wallet data.
- Store copies of your recovery phrase in several secure locations to safeguard against loss or damage.

With a strong foundation of protective measures and consistent habits, you can significantly reduce the risks associated with managing digital assets and keep your cryptocurrency safe from prying hands.

2.3 TROUBLESHOOTING COMMON WALLET ISSUES

Navigating the world of cryptocurrency wallets can sometimes feel like navigating a maze. You're not alone if you encounter some bumps along the way. One of the most common issues users face is losing access due to **forgotten passwords or misplaced seed phrases**. Without these, accessing your funds becomes nearly impossible. Many wallets offer password recovery options but usually require the crucial seed phrase. Ensure your email is linked to your wallet, as some providers may let you reset your password through email verification. Always familiarize yourself with the specific recovery processes of your wallet provider, as they can differ. Once you select a wallet, take time to understand the available recovery options should you lose your password or seed phrase. This proactive approach can help you prepare for potential losses.

Transaction errors can also throw a wrench in your crypto dealings. Imagine sending money, but it never arrives, or seeing it stuck in limbo. This can sometimes happen due to network congestion or incorrect transaction fees. If your transaction hangs in the balance, check that you've set the appropriate fee. Sometimes, increasing it can expedite the process. Always confirm that you're using the correct wallet address. A single typo can send your funds to an unknown location, and sadly, there's no recovery in such cases. For processing issues, consult your wallet's transaction history and blockchain explorers like Blockchain.com Explorer or Etherscan to track the status. This helps pinpoint the exact problem and determine if further action is needed.

For those persistent issues that seem beyond your troubleshooting skills, there's no shame in reaching out for help. Official wallet support forums are a treasure trove of information, often hosting solutions to similar problems others have faced. These platforms connect you with both the wallet's technical support team and a community of users who've likely faced the same hurdles. Community user guides and discussion boards can also be invaluable, as they often contain practical tips and personal experiences that can guide you to a solution.

Most cryptocurrency wallet issues can be avoided by securing private keys, keeping wallets updated, and double-checking transactions before sending. To prevent irreversible losses, always use official wallet apps, enable security features, and store seed phrases securely in multiple locations.

Back up your wallet regularly, ensuring you can recover access even if your device fails or is lost. Regularly updating these backups is crucial, especially if your wallet undergoes any changes. This ensures that your backup is always current and can be relied upon in an emergency.

Nobody likes to think about problems, but having a plan in place makes all the difference. Regularly review your backup strategy to ensure it's still effective. It's easy to neglect this once everything's running smoothly, but vigilance is key. By staying proactive, you'll easily navigate wallet woes and keep your digital assets safe and sound.

2.4 WALLET QUIZ: TEST YOUR KNOWLEDGE

As we wrap up this chapter on choosing and securing your cryptocurrency wallet, it's time to put your newfound knowledge to the test. You've learned a lot about different wallet types, how to set them up, and ways to keep them secure. Now, let's see how much you remember with this short quiz. This isn't just about testing what you know; it's about reinforcing these critical concepts. Consider each question carefully, and remember that understanding these basics is crucial for confidently managing your digital assets.

True or False

1. A hardware wallet is always connected to the internet, making it less secure than a software wallet. (True/False)
2. Using a strong password and enabling two-factor authentication are optional steps that can be skipped if your wallet is backed up regularly. (True/False)
3. If you lose your recovery phrase, you can still access your wallet if you remember your password. (True/False)
4. Phishing attacks can be avoided by only downloading wallet software from official websites. (True/False)

Multiple Choice

5. Which of the following is a feature of a mobile wallet?
   - A) Requires physical connection to a computer
   - B) Accessible on the go via smartphone
   - C) Stores cryptocurrency offline
6. What is the primary advantage of using a cold storage solution?
   - A) Fast transaction processing
   - B) Enhanced security by keeping keys offline
   - C) Free access to all cryptocurrencies
7. What should you verify before initiating a transaction?
   - A) The color of your wallet interface
   - B) The accuracy of the wallet address
   - C) The time of day
8. A wallet that combines features of both hot and cold storage is known as a:
   - A) Paper wallet
   - B) Hybrid wallet
   - C) Mobile wallet

Answers & Explanations

1. False
   - *Explanation:* Hardware wallets are not connected to the internet when not in use, which makes them more secure than software wallets.
2. False
   - *Explanation:* Strong passwords and two-factor authentication are crucial security measures that should always be implemented.
3. False
   - *Explanation:* The recovery phrase is crucial for accessing your wallet if you lose your password or device.

4. True
    - *Explanation:* Ensuring you download software from trusted sources reduces the risk of phishing attacks.
5. B) Accessible on the go via smartphone
    - *Explanation:* Mobile wallets allow users to manage cryptocurrency conveniently through their smartphones.
6. B) Enhanced security by keeping keys offline
    - *Explanation:* Cold storage solutions provide enhanced security by keeping private keys offline, reducing hacking risks.
7. B) The accuracy of the wallet address
    - *Explanation:* Always double-check the wallet address before sending funds to avoid irreversible losses.
8. B) Hybrid wallet
    - *Explanation:* Hybrid wallets offer a combination of hot and cold storage features for greater flexibility and security.

Final Thoughts

Quiz results are more than just numbers; they're a chance to see where you shine and where you might need more review. If you found some questions challenging, don't worry – this is all part of the learning process. Go back to the sections that felt tricky and give them another read. The more you familiarize yourself with these concepts, the more comfortable you'll become with making informed decisions about your cryptocurrency investments.

Now that you've tackled the essentials of choosing and securing your wallet, you're well-equipped to handle the basics of cryptocurrency management. With this foundation laid, it's time to explore the broader landscape of cryptocurrency exchanges and trading strategies. Each step you take builds on the last, and before you know it, you'll be navigating the world of digital assets with confidence and skill.

CHAPTER 3
NAVIGATING CRYPTOCURRENCY EXCHANGES

PICTURE THIS: You're at a bustling marketplace, surrounded by stalls offering every imaginable product. But instead of fruit and vegetables, this market offers digital assets – cryptocurrencies. Choosing the right stall, or in this case, the right exchange, can make all the difference in your trading experience. Cryptocurrency exchanges are the digital equivalent of these stalls, acting as platforms where you can buy, sell, and trade various cryptocurrencies. With hundreds of exchanges out there, it's essential to know how to pick one that is trustworthy and suitable for your needs. This chapter will guide you through the maze of options, helping you identify key factors to consider when selecting an exchange.

When evaluating cryptocurrency exchanges, regulatory compliance is a crucial factor. Exchanges that adhere to regulations are typically more trustworthy and provide a level of protection for your investments. They are often subject to audits and must follow strict guidelines to ensure transparency and security. Look for exchanges licensed by reputable regulatory bodies, which indicates a commitment to operating within legal frameworks. For example, the Financial Crimes Enforcement Network (FinCEN) requires crypto companies engaged in money transmission, including exchanges, to register as a Money Services Business (MSB). This registration ensures compliance with anti-money laundering (AML) and Know Your Customer (KYC) laws. Regulatory considerations, including resources and websites for regulatory agencies, will be discussed in detail in a later chapter.

Security measures are another critical factor to consider. Reliable exchanges employ robust security protocols, such as SSL encryption and two-factor authentication, to protect user information and funds from cyber threats. A strong reputation, backed by positive user reviews, can also be a good indicator of an exchange's reliability and quality of service.

Before diving into trading, it's vital to conduct thorough research, including checking for any history of security breaches, as past incidents can signal potential vulnerabilities. Assessing an exchange's financial stability is also important, as financially sound exchanges are less likely to experience disruptions or insolvency. Take the time to read up on user experiences and expert reviews to get a sense of how the exchange operates and treats its customers. This due diligence will help you avoid falling into the trap of unreliable platforms, where the risks of losing funds or encountering data breaches are high.

Deciding between centralized and decentralized exchanges can be like choosing between a guided tour and a solo adventure. **Centralized exchanges**, like Binance and Coinbase, act as intermediaries between buyers and sellers, offering user-friendly interfaces, higher liquidity, and customer support. They hold your private keys, which means you trust them with your funds. While providing convenience and a wide range of cryptocurrencies, they also have potential downsides, such as security vulnerabilities and regulatory oversight.

On the other hand, **decentralized exchanges** like Uniswap operate on blockchain technology, allowing peer-to-peer transactions without intermediaries. They offer greater privacy and control over your assets but come with lower liquidity and a steeper learning curve for beginners.

Several exchanges have built strong reputations for reliability and security. Coinbase is often recommended for beginners due to its user-friendly platform and strong security measures. It's a great starting point for those new to crypto trading. Binance offers a wide selection of coins and features for more experienced traders, making it a popular choice for those looking to explore a diverse range of digital assets. Kraken is known for its advanced features and robust security, appealing to traders who require more sophisticated tools and options.

Security features are paramount when selecting an exchange. Two-factor authentication is a must, as it adds an extra layer of protection for your account. Some exchanges also offer insurance policies for digital assets, providing additional peace of mind in the event of unforeseen incidents. A user-friendly interface can significantly impact your trading experience. Exchanges with intuitive navigation and mobile app availability make managing your trades and monitoring your portfolio easier. Liquidity and trading volume are also important considerations, as exchanges with high liquidity facilitate smoother trades and better pricing. High daily trading volumes often indicate strong liquidity, which can impact the speed and efficiency of order execution.

3.1 THE IMPORTANCE OF KYC AND VERIFICATION PROCESSES

Navigating the world of cryptocurrency exchanges, you'll inevitably encounter the term KYC, which stands for "Know Your Customer." It's more than just a buzzword; it's a foundational element in the crypto exchange ecosystem. At its core, KYC is about verifying the identity of users. This process is crucial for maintaining the integrity and security of exchanges. By verifying identities, exchanges can help prevent fraudulent activities, such as money laundering and other illicit practices. It's like showing your ID when opening a bank account. This verification is part of a broader commitment to anti-money laundering (AML) compliance. AML measures are vital for keeping exchanges in line with legal requirements and protecting them from being used for criminal purposes. The benefits of KYC are clear: enhanced security, increased trustworthiness, and a safer environment for everyone involved.

The KYC process requires you to provide specific documentation. You must present a government-issued ID, like a driver's license or passport, as proof of identity. In some cases, exchanges may also ask for proof of address, such as a utility bill or bank statement. This information helps exchanges confirm that you are who you claim to be. Once you've gathered your documents, you'll usually upload them directly to the exchange's platform. The exchange then verifies your identity and address through their internal processes. The timeline for verification can vary, ranging from a few hours to a couple of days, depending on the exchange and the volume of applications they receive. Sometimes, documents are rejected because they are expired, unclear, or do not meet the exchange's criteria. In such instances, you must resubmit the required documentation as specified.

A common concern with KYC is privacy. Many users worry about how their personal data will be handled and stored. It's a legitimate concern, and choosing exchanges with strong privacy policies is essential. Reputable exchanges employ advanced data encryption techniques to protect your personal information from unauthorized access. They also have strict data storage practices to ensure your information is secure. Furthermore, users typically have rights regarding their data, including access, correction, and deletion, depending on the jurisdiction. These rights allow you to manage your personal information and how it's used.

While KYC might seem like a hurdle, it serves a critical purpose in the crypto landscape. By verifying identities, exchanges can create a more secure and reliable trading environment. This not only benefits the exchanges themselves but also protects users from potential risks associated with anonymous trading. With a solid understanding of KYC and its role in the crypto ecosystem, you can confidently approach the verification process, knowing that it's a step towards a safer and more transparent trading experience.

3.2 COMPARING EXCHANGE FEATURES AND FEES

Navigating the diverse landscape of cryptocurrency exchanges can be like maneuvering through a crowded marketplace, with numerous vendors vying for your attention. It can be challenging to distinguish the advantages of one exchange over another. Each platform offers unique features that can significantly impact your trading experience. A user-friendly interface is crucial, as it can make the difference between a smooth, intuitive trading process and a confusing, frustrating one. Look for exchanges that prioritize ease of use, offering clear layouts and accessible navigation to help you execute trades efficiently. The range of supported cryptocurrencies is another key consideration. Some exchanges offer a vast array of digital assets, giving you the flexibility to diversify your portfolio with established coins and promising altcoins.

Additionally, consider the available trading pairs and liquidity. Trading pairs refer to two different digital assets that can be exchanged on a trading platform where traders can swap one cryptocurrency for another. An exchange with high liquidity ensures you can swiftly buy or sell assets without significantly affecting the market price since values can fluctuate significantly in a short time. This is critical for active traders looking to capitalize on market movements. Large, well-known exchanges (e.g., Binance and Coinbase) have more liquidity than smaller platforms. The higher the daily trading volume, the more liquid the asset. Exploring these aspects can help you choose an exchange that aligns with your trading needs and goals.

Understanding the fee structures of cryptocurrency exchanges is crucial. Every exchange has its own set of fees, and these can quickly add up, impacting your overall profitability. There are various cryptocurrency trading fees, including exchange, withdrawal and deposit, network, and spread fees.

Trading fees (exchange fees) are the most common and typically come in two forms: maker and taker fees. **Maker fees** are charged when placing a limit order that adds liquidity to the market. The order is to buy or sell at a specific price and does not occur immediately. On the other hand, **taker fees** are imposed on traders who place orders that are immediately executed at the market price. Takers remove liquidity because the transaction is immediate. Both incur different fees, and it's essential to grasp how these will affect your trades.

Deposit and withdrawal fees are another consideration. Some exchanges charge a percentage or flat fee for moving funds in and out. If you plan to trade frequently, these fees can eat into your profits. Additionally, exchanges sometimes charge **inactivity fees** to penalize accounts that remain dormant for extended periods. So, if you're a long-term holder, ensure you're not caught off guard by unexpected charges. By being mindful of these costs, you can make informed decisions that maximize your returns.

Fees can make or break your trading strategy, especially if you're operating on tight margins. For short-term trades, where profits can be slim, high fees may significantly erode your gains. Long-term investors might feel less of an impact, but keeping an eye on expenses is still crucial. To minimize fee costs, consider strategies like consolidating trades to reduce the frequency of transactions or choosing exchanges with more favorable fee structures. Some exchanges offer fee discounts for holding their native tokens or participating in loyalty programs, which could make a difference over time. When selecting an exchange, align it with your trading habits, whether you're a frequent trader or a buy-and-hold investor, ensuring the fee structure suits your approach.

Selecting the right exchange is not a one-size-fits-all decision. Consider how often you plan to trade and the specific assets you're interested in. An exchange with a broad range of cryptocurrencies might be more appealing if you're keen on exploring new altcoins. For those who trade frequently, prioritize exchanges with low transaction fees and high liquidity to enhance efficiency. Take advantage of online exchange comparison sites to evaluate features and fees side by side. These resources can provide valuable insights into each exchange's offerings, allowing you to weigh their pros and cons effectively. User forums and review platforms are also helpful, offering first-hand accounts of other traders' experiences to guide your choice.

Finding the right exchange involves balancing many factors, but with careful consideration and the correct information, you can choose a platform that complements your trading style and goals. By exploring different options and understanding the intricacies of fees and features, you can enhance your trading experience and improve your chances of success in the vibrant world of cryptocurrency.

3.3 AVOIDING EXCHANGE SCAMS: RED FLAGS TO WATCH FOR

Imagine walking through an online marketplace filled with promises of easy riches and guaranteed profits. Fraudulent exchanges lurk in this bustling digital space, waiting to deceive the unsuspecting. Fake exchange websites often mimic the appearance of legitimate platforms, complete with fabricated logos and professional designs. They might even use domain names that closely resemble those of reputable exchanges, hoping to trick you into entering your login details. Once you do, they can gain access to your personal information or, worse, your hard-earned funds. Phishing emails and messages are another common tactic. These communications might urge you to click on a link to "verify your account" or "claim a reward," only leading you to a harmful site designed to capture your sensitive information.

As you navigate this landscape, certain red flags can help you spot potential scams. Be wary of exchanges that make unrealistic promises of high returns with little to no risk. As the saying goes, if something sounds too good to be true, it probably is. A lack of transparency in company information is another warning sign. Legitimate exchanges will provide details about their team, location, and regulatory status. If you find yourself struggling to unearth this information, proceed with caution. Similarly, exchanges that are vague about their fees and policies might be hiding something. Always seek out platforms that are upfront about their operational details, as opacity can often signal dubious intentions.

To protect yourself, verifying an exchange's legitimacy is paramount. Begin by checking for regulatory certifications, which can lend credibility to an exchange. Most reputable exchanges will proudly display their certifications and affiliations. Additionally, verify the domain authenticity. Scammers often create websites with URLs that look similar to well-known exchanges, so pay attention to any slight discrepancies. Reviewing customer feedback is also invaluable. Look for reviews from other users, especially on independent platforms, to gauge their experiences and identify potential issues. This step can provide insights into the reliability and reputation of an exchange, guiding you toward safer choices.

Real-world examples of exchange scams serve as cautionary tales. The collapse of Mt. Gox, once the world's largest Bitcoin exchange, resulted in the loss of hundreds of thousands of Bitcoins and highlighted the catastrophic impact of security failures. Similarly, Bitconnect, a well-known Ponzi scheme, promised incredible returns through a lending program, only to collapse and leave investors with significant losses. These cases underscore the importance of due diligence and vigilance when choosing an exchange. They remind us that even seemingly successful platforms can be vulnerable to mismanagement or malicious intent, leading to devastating consequences for users.

As you continue exploring the world of cryptocurrency exchanges, keep these cautionary tips in mind. By staying informed and attentive to red flags, you can significantly reduce your risk of falling victim to fraudulent schemes. Remember, knowledge is your best defense.

3.4 EXCHANGE QUIZ: TEST YOUR KNOWLEDGE

Now that we've discussed navigating the world of cryptocurrency exchanges, it's time to put your knowledge to the test. This quiz reinforces what you've learned and highlights areas you might want to revisit. Think of it as a friendly challenge rather than a daunting test. We'll cover various aspects of exchanges, focusing on some of the critical topics we've explored.

True or False

1. Centralized exchanges are managed by central authorities, while decentralized exchanges allow peer-to-peer transactions without intermediaries. (True/False)
2. Two-factor authentication is an optional security measure that doesn't significantly enhance your account's security. (True/False)
3. An exchange that guarantees high returns with no risk is likely legitimate. (True/False)

Multiple Choice

4. Which type of exchange typically offers higher liquidity and user-friendly interfaces?
   - A) Centralized exchanges
   - B) Decentralized exchanges
   - C) Both offer similar experiences
5. Which of the following is a common security feature offered by reputable exchanges?
   - A) Daily password changes
   - B) Insurance policies for digital assets
   - C) Free trading fees
6. Which of the following fees is typically charged when you trade on an exchange?
   - A) Withdrawal fees
   - B) Maker/taker fees
   - C) Monthly subscription fees
7. What should you do if an exchange lacks transparency about its team and location?
   - A) Proceed with caution and conduct further research
   - B) Trust the exchange based on its website design
   - C) Ignore these details as they're irrelevant
8. Which of the following is a common tactic used by fraudulent exchanges?
   - A) Offering educational resources
   - B) Phishing emails and messages
   - C) Hosting community forums

Answers & Explanations

1. True
   - *Explanation*: Centralized exchanges involve a central authority that manages operations and usually requires users to comply with regulations like KYC. Decentralized exchanges operate on blockchain technology, allowing users to trade directly without an intermediary.

2. False
    - *Explanation*: Two-factor authentication adds an extra layer of security by requiring a second form of verification, making it much harder for unauthorized users to access your account.
3. False
    - *Explanation*: Any platform that promises guaranteed high returns with no risk is likely a scam.
4. A) Centralized exchanges
    - *Explanation*: These platforms often have more resources to support liquidity and user experience enhancements, making them more accessible for newcomers.
5. B) Insurance policies for digital assets
    - *Explanation*: Some exchanges offer insurance to protect against losses due to unforeseen incidents, providing additional peace of mind.
6. B) Maker/taker fees
    - *Explanation:* These fees apply when you place orders on the platform, with makers adding liquidity and takers removing it.
7. A) Proceed with caution and conduct further research
    - *Explanation*: Transparency is crucial, and a lack of it should be a warning sign.
8. B) Phishing emails and messages
    - *Explanation*: Scammers often use phishing tactics to trick users into revealing sensitive information.

You've worked through the intricacies of cryptocurrency exchanges, gaining insights into how they function and what to watch out for. These platforms are gateways to the exciting world of digital assets, and understanding their nuances is crucial for making informed decisions. As we move forward, keep these lessons in mind, and let's continue our exploration of cryptocurrency.

CHAPTER 4
DEVELOPING A PERSONALIZED TRADING PLAN

IMAGINE SETTING sail on the open sea without a map or a destination in mind. The journey might be exciting at first, but without direction, you risk drifting aimlessly. This is what trading without a plan can feel like – exciting yet chaotic. Establishing a personalized trading plan is your map, helping you navigate the turbulent waters of cryptocurrency trading. It provides structure and purpose, ensuring every decision aligns with your financial goals. By setting clear investment objectives, you can chart a course that guides your trading activities and measures your success along the way.

Having specific investment goals is crucial for several reasons. They serve as a compass, guiding your trading decisions and keeping you focused amidst the noise and volatility of the market. Think of your goals as the anchor that keeps you grounded, preventing impulsive decisions driven by market hype or fear. Short-term profit targets help you seize timely opportunities, capitalize on favorable market conditions, and secure immediate gains. On the other hand, long-term wealth accumulation focuses on building a robust portfolio, allowing your investments to grow and compound over time. Both types of goals have their place, and having a mix can provide a balanced approach that caters to your unique circumstances.

Establishing realistic and achievable goals requires careful consideration. One effective method is to use the **SMART criteria** – *Specific, Measurable, Achievable, Relevant, and Time-bound.*

S – Specific – Begin by identifying what you want to achieve, whether it's a specific profit percentage or a milestone like funding a major purchase.

M – Measurable – Make sure your goals are measurable so you can track your progress along the way.

A – Achievable – They should also be achievable based on your current resources and market conditions, avoiding overly ambitious targets that could lead to disappointment. Set targets that are realistic given your current resources, knowledge, and market conditions. Overly ambitious goals can lead to frustration.

R – Relevant – Ensure your goals are relevant and align with your broader financial objectives.

T – Time-bound – Establish a deadline to create urgency and keep yourself accountable.

This approach provides clarity and direction. By applying the SMART framework, you give your goals structure and direction – transforming vague aspirations into a clear plan for success.

Investment goals can vary widely, reflecting diverse motivations and outcomes. **Growth-oriented** goals focus on increasing your capital through strategic investments, often involving higher-risk assets with the potential for substantial returns. This approach suits those willing to embrace volatility for the chance to amplify their wealth. On the other hand, **income-focused** objectives prioritize generating consistent returns, often through dividends or interest, providing a steady stream of income. This strategy might appeal to those seeking financial stability or supplementing their earnings without taking excessive risk. Both types of goals are valid, and your choice depends on your financial situation, risk tolerance, and long-term aspirations.

Regular goal reassessment and adjustment are vital for staying on track. The cryptocurrency market is dynamic, influenced by economic shifts, regulatory changes, and technological advancements. As these factors evolve, so too should your goals. Periodically review your objectives to ensure they remain relevant and achievable, adapting them to reflect new market conditions or personal milestones. This flexibility allows you to stay responsive and resilient, enhancing your ability to navigate the ever-changing landscape. Revisiting your goals also provides an opportunity to celebrate achievements, boosting your confidence and motivation.

Evaluating and refining your trading plan is an ongoing process. As you gain experience trading, you can extract valuable insights from analyzing past trades. What strategies worked well, and where did you encounter challenges? Use these reflections to identify areas for improvement and refine your approach. Incorporate new tools and techniques as you continue learning, staying informed about market trends and innovations. Consider setting performance benchmarks that serve as milestones, helping you gauge your progress and adjust your strategies accordingly. Maintaining a proactive mindset and embracing continuous improvement can optimize your trading plan for success.

Reflection Section: Crafting Your Investment Goals

Take a moment to reflect on your financial aspirations. What do you want to achieve through cryptocurrency trading? Write down two short-term and two long-term goals, ensuring they align with the SMART criteria. Consider how these goals fit within your broader financial picture and how they might evolve over time. This exercise will help you crystallize your objectives and set the stage for a focused and successful trading journey.

4.1 IDENTIFYING YOUR RISK TOLERANCE

Risk tolerance is a crucial aspect of trading that often gets overlooked in the excitement of entering the crypto market. It's your ability and willingness to endure the ups and downs of investment values, and it plays a significant role in shaping your trading strategies and decisions. Think of risk tolerance as the barometer of how much volatility you can stomach. It's not just about numbers or potential losses but also about your emotional capacity to handle fluctuations. Your **financial risk capacity** is determined by your financial situation – how much you can afford to lose without impacting your lifestyle; while your **emotional risk capacity** is about how well you cope with the stress of uncertainty. Together, these components form the backbone of your **risk tolerance**, guiding the types of investments you engage in and the strategies you employ.

To understand your personal risk tolerance, start by reflecting on your comfort level with potential losses. Consider using risk assessment questionnaires that ask about your reactions to market fluctuations, past experiences, and investment preferences. These tools can help you gauge where you stand on the risk spectrum. Another approach is to analyze your historical financial behavior. If you have investment experience, think of how you've reacted to past market changes or investment challenges. If you've invested in the stock market in the past, did you panic and sell, or did you ride the waves calmly? Your past behavior can offer valuable insights into your risk tolerance. This self-reflection process may reveal whether you're naturally inclined towards risk-seeking or risk-averse decisions, helping you tailor your investment approach accordingly.

Your risk tolerance significantly impacts how you allocate assets in your portfolio. A conservative risk tolerance might lead you to favor more stable, lower-risk investments, such as established cryptocurrencies like Bitcoin or Ethereum. These assets tend to have less volatility compared to lesser-known altcoins. Conversely, if you have a high-risk tolerance, you might be more inclined to explore aggressive asset allocation involving a mix of high-potential altcoins and emerging technologies. This approach can offer substantial rewards, but it also comes with increased risk. Understanding where you fall on this spectrum lets you make informed decisions about which assets to include in your portfolio, ensuring that your investments align with your comfort level.

Aligning your risk tolerance with your financial goals is vital. It helps ensure that the risks you take are consistent with the outcomes you desire. Balancing risk with expected returns means evaluating whether the potential gains justify the level of risk involved. If your financial goals are more conservative, such as preserving capital for future needs, it might be wise to reduce exposure to high-risk assets.

Conversely, if you aim for substantial growth, you might be willing to accept more volatility in pursuit of higher returns. Adjusting your risk exposure over time is important. As you reach certain milestones or market conditions shift, reassess your risk tolerance and make necessary adjustments. This adaptability ensures that your investment strategy remains aligned with your current situation and long-term objectives.

4.2 SELECTING TRADING STRATEGIES: DAY, SWING, AND LONG-TERM

In the vast world of cryptocurrency trading, picking the right strategy can feel like choosing the right pair of shoes for a long hike. You want something that fits your style, supports your journey, and helps you reach your destination comfortably. Let's explore the three principal trading strategies: day trading, swing trading, and long-term investing.

Day trading is like the sprinter of the trading world. It involves making numerous trades within a single day, relying heavily on technical analysis and charting systems. The goal is to capitalize on small price movements, closing all positions by the end of the day. This strategy demands a high level of attention and a sophisticated trading setup. It's fast-paced and high-risk but offers the potential for quick profits. However, it can also lead to significant financial losses, especially for beginners. The time commitment required is substantial, often turning day trading into a full-time endeavor. So, if you thrive in a dynamic environment and can handle the pressure, day trading might be your fit.

Swing trading, on the other hand, is more like a marathon. It focuses on capturing gains over a period of days to weeks, taking advantage of market swings. This strategy allows you to maintain other commitments, as it requires less constant monitoring compared to day trading. Swing trading offers a balance of risk and reward, with the potential for more significant returns due to longer holding periods. However, it also carries the risk of more significant losses if the market moves against you. Swing trading might not have the adrenaline rush of day trading, but its methodical approach may suit those who prefer a steadier pace. Swing trading requires patience and a keen eye for emerging trends.

Long-term investing is like planting a tree and watching it grow. It's about stability and growth over time, focusing on the potential of cryptocurrencies to appreciate in value. This strategy involves buying and holding assets for months or even years, riding out market volatility. It's suitable for those who prefer a hands-off approach with the patience to weather market fluctuations. Long-term investing is less stressful, offering peace of mind and the potential for significant wealth accumulation. However, it requires a strong belief in the future of cryptocurrencies and the discipline to stay the course despite short-term setbacks.

Choosing the right strategy depends on several factors. Consider your time availability – day trading demands a full-time commitment, while swing trading and long-term investing offer more flexibility. Assess your financial resources, as day trading often involves high transaction fees that can eat into profits. Emotional resilience is also key, as each strategy presents its unique challenges. Day traders must handle rapid decisions and pressure, while swing traders and long-term investors need patience and the ability to stay calm during market downturns.

Sometimes, your circumstances or goals may change, prompting a shift in strategy. Transitioning smoothly is important. Start by making incremental adaptations, such as gradually increasing the holding period of your trades if you're moving from day trading to swing trading. Consider hybridizing strategies, blending elements of different approaches to create one that suits your evolving needs. For example, you might combine swing trading with aspects of long-term investing, holding onto promising assets for extended periods while taking advantage of short-term opportunities. Adjust and experiment while keeping your overall goals and risk tolerance in mind.

4.3 IMPLEMENTING YOUR PLAN: START SMALL AND BEGIN WITH PAPER TRADING

When you first step into the world of cryptocurrency trading, it's easy to feel like you're wading into deep waters. The idea of starting small might seem counterintuitive, especially when you hear stories of people making big bucks overnight. But diving in with limited capital exposure is a wise choice. Think of it like testing the waters with your toes before plunging in. By beginning with a modest investment, you minimize your risk while gaining valuable hands-on experience. This approach allows you to learn through practice, understand market mechanics, and build confidence without the stress of significant financial loss looming over you.

One of the best ways to dip your toes into trading without the risk of losing real money is by starting with **paper trading**. This tool allows you to simulate trades, giving you a sandbox to experiment in. Imagine having the freedom to test strategies, monitor hypothetical outcomes, and refine your skills without fearing financial repercussions. Simulated trading platforms provide a safe environment to explore the intricacies of trading. By engaging in paper trading, you can build the confidence to face the real market. It's like having a practice run before the main event, helping you understand how different strategies play out in various market conditions.

Setting up a paper trading account is an excellent first step towards understanding the market dynamics. Start by choosing a platform that suits your needs. Options like TradingView and Binance offer user-friendly interfaces that cater to beginners. Once you've picked a platform, configure your account settings and preferences. Start by setting a virtual balance that mirrors what you would realistically invest. This setup will give you a better feel for managing your resources. As you navigate the platform, familiarize yourself with its features, such as charting tools and performance tracking. These tools will be invaluable when you transition to live trading.

When you're ready to move from paper trading to live trading, a gradual transition is key. Begin by slowly increasing your investment size rather than jumping in with your entire capital. This method helps you acclimate to the emotional rollercoaster that can accompany trading real money. Recognizing that actual losses are possible prepares you mentally, reducing the shock and stress that can lead to rash decisions. It's essential to remain patient and avoid rushing the process. Think of it as gradually increasing your workout intensity rather than jumping straight into a marathon. This way, you build a robust foundation for long-term trading success.

Continuous reflection and plan adjustment are essential components of a successful trading strategy. Regular performance reviews allow you to assess your trades, identify patterns, and learn from both successes and mistakes. Take the time to analyze what worked and what didn't, and use these insights to optimize your strategy. The market is ever-changing, and adapting to new trends or shifts is essential to stay ahead. This iterative process ensures your trading plan remains dynamic and responsive to personal growth and market conditions. Embrace the journey of learning and adaptation, knowing that each step forward brings you closer to your trading goals.

4.4 TRADING PLAN CHECKLIST

Creating a trading plan is like crafting a blueprint for a new home – you need a solid foundation before you begin. Use this checklist to develop a strategy that aligns with your goals and resources.

- **Define Your Motivation**
    - Are you drawn to cryptocurrency for its technology or financial gains?
    - What are your short-term and long-term trading objectives?
- **Assess Your Resources**
    - How much time can you realistically dedicate to trading?
    - What is your available capital, and how much are you comfortable risking?
- **Select Trading Tools & Platforms**
    - Have you researched and chosen a reliable trading platform?

  - Do you need additional tools, educational courses, or software to improve your trading skills?
- **Implement Risk Management Strategies**
  - How will you protect your investments (e.g., stop-loss orders, portfolio diversification)?
  - How will you handle losses and maintain discipline during market volatility?
- **Establish Performance Evaluation Criteria**
  - What benchmarks and performance indicators will you use to assess your trades?
  - How often will you review and refine your trading strategy?
- **Stay Informed**
  - What sources of market analysis and news will you rely on?
  - How will you continue your education to adapt to the evolving cryptocurrency landscape?

By following this checklist, you can create a trading plan that is structured, adaptable, and aligned with your financial goals. Remember that building a trading plan is just the beginning. Like any well-laid plan, regular attention and revision are required to stay effective.

CHAPTER 5
BUILDING A CRYPTOCURRENCY PORTFOLIO

IMAGINE you're putting together a jigsaw puzzle. Each piece, unique in its shape and color, contributes to the bigger picture. In the world of crypto investing, diversification is akin to this puzzle. Each cryptocurrency represents a distinct piece, and your goal is to fit them together to create a balanced and resilient portfolio. Diversification isn't just a buzzword; it's a strategy that can shield you from the unpredictable nature of the cryptocurrency market. By spreading your investments across different assets, you reduce the risk of a single point of failure. This approach is essential for building a sturdy financial future in the world of digital currencies.

Diversifying your crypto portfolio involves more than just picking random coins. It requires a thoughtful approach to asset selection. Consider investing in a mix of renowned cryptocurrencies like Bitcoin and Ethereum, along with promising altcoins that offer different technological innovations and use cases. These altcoins could focus on areas like smart contracts, decentralized finance, or even gaming. Including stablecoins in your portfolio is another smart move. Stablecoins, like Tether and USD Coin, maintain a consistent value, providing a cushion against the market's volatility. Having a portion of your portfolio in stablecoins creates a safe harbor for your investments, mitigating the impact of market swings.

When it comes to effective diversification, there are practical strategies you can employ. Allocating a percentage of your portfolio to emerging projects can be a game-changer. These projects are often at the forefront of innovation, offering potential for significant returns as they gain traction. However, balancing these high-risk, high-reward assets with more stable investments is essential. Your portfolio should reflect a mix of high-risk and low-risk assets, creating a spectrum that aligns with your risk tolerance and investment goals.

The benefits of diversification are manifold. By spreading your investments across various assets, you protect yourself from market downturns in specific sectors. If one asset underperforms, others in your portfolio may counterbalance the loss. This protective buffer enhances your portfolio's resilience, much like a well-built bridge that withstands strong winds. Additionally, diversification allows you to capture growth in different market segments. As various sectors within the cryptocurrency landscape evolve, your diversified portfolio positions you to benefit from these shifts, potentially leading to long-term gains.

However, diversification isn't without its pitfalls. Over-diversification can dilute returns, as spreading your investments too thinly may result in negligible gains. It's crucial to strike a balance, ensuring that each asset in your portfolio has a meaningful impact. Another common mistake is neglecting due diligence on individual assets. Each cryptocurrency should be carefully researched and evaluated, considering factors like technology, market demand, and team expertise. Ignoring this step is like buying a car without checking its engine, potentially leading to unforeseen issues down the road.

Reflection Section: Evaluating Your Diversification Strategy

Take a moment to assess your current diversification strategy. Reflect on the following questions:

- Are your investments spread across different types of cryptocurrencies?
- Have you included stablecoins to balance volatility?

- Are you balancing high-risk and low-risk assets?
- Are you conducting thorough research on each asset?

Jot down your answers and identify any areas for improvement. This exercise will help refine your approach, ensuring your portfolio is well-diversified and aligned with your investment goals.

5.1 RISK ASSESSMENT: BALANCING HIGH AND LOW VOLATILITY ASSETS

When we talk about volatility in the context of investments, we're referring to the degree of variation in the price of an asset over time. It's a measure of how much an asset's price can jump up or down. For cryptocurrency, volatility is particularly pronounced. The more volatile an investment, the riskier it is. An asset with higher volatility has the potential for higher returns, but it also has the potential for more significant losses over a shorter period. This volatility can make crypto exciting but also nerve-wracking.

Volatility indexes, such as CVI (Crypto Volatility Index) and CVIX (Cryptocurrency VIX), are tools used to track these fluctuations. They give you a snapshot of how turbulent the market is, helping you gauge the level of risk involved. **Historical price fluctuations** are another critical aspect to consider. They provide insights into how an asset has behaved in the past, which can be a useful predictor for future movements. By understanding these patterns, you can better anticipate how your portfolio might react to market changes.

In the world of cryptocurrency, not all coins are created equal when it comes to volatility. Bitcoin, often seen as the benchmark, tends to be less volatile compared to many altcoins. Its larger market cap and widespread adoption lend it a degree of stability, at least relative to the crypto space. On the other hand, emerging altcoins can be highly volatile. These newer coins might experience rapid price swings as they react to market speculation, news, or development updates. While these fluctuations can offer opportunities for significant gains, they also come with heightened risk. It's like walking a tightrope without a net – thrilling but dangerous. Understanding the volatility levels of different cryptocurrencies helps you manage potential risks in your portfolio, ensuring you're not overly exposed to assets that might cause wild price swings.

Balancing volatility within your portfolio is crucial to achieving stability while still pursuing growth. One effective strategy is to allocate a portion of your portfolio to stablecoins. These coins provide a buffer against the unpredictable nature of other cryptocurrencies. The presence of stablecoins in your portfolio acts as an anchor, providing stability and reducing the overall volatility of your investments. While no investment is without risk, incorporating stablecoins can create a more balanced and resilient portfolio in the ever-changing landscape of cryptocurrency.

Hedging strategies can also play a role in managing volatility. Using techniques such as buying options or futures contracts, you can offset potential losses in your portfolio, much like a financial safety net. These strategies require a bit more knowledge and skill but can be invaluable for those looking to mitigate risk.

5.2 LONG-TERM VS. SHORT-TERM INVESTMENTS: PROS AND CONS

When navigating the cryptocurrency landscape, choosing between long-term and short-term investment strategies is like deciding between planting a tree and picking flowers. Each has its benefits and challenges; understanding these can help you tailor your approach. Long-term investments in crypto are like planting a sturdy tree that grows over time. The potential for compound growth is a significant advantage here. As you hold onto assets like Bitcoin or Ethereum, you give them a chance to appreciate in value, riding the waves of market cycles and benefiting from the overall upward trends. This approach requires patience and a belief in the enduring value of the cryptocurrency you're investing in. However, it also means weathering market downturns, which can test your resolve.

On the other hand, short-term investments are more like picking flowers – quick, often rewarding, but requiring constant attention. This strategy involves capitalizing on the volatile nature of cryptocurrencies, particularly altcoins. These assets can experience rapid price changes, offering opportunities for quick profits if you time your trades well. However, this approach comes with its own set of challenges. The market's unpredictable swings demand discipline and a keen eye for trends. It's a dynamic strategy, better suited for those who thrive in fast-paced environments and have the time to monitor the market closely.

There are specific scenarios where each strategy shines. Long-term holding is ideal for major cryptocurrencies with established track records and steady growth. If your goal is to build wealth over time and you're comfortable with the ups and downs of the market, this approach might be for you. It allows you to take a step back, focus on other aspects of your life, and let your investment grow. Conversely, short-term trading can be lucrative in a volatile market, especially when dealing with emerging altcoins. When the market is experiencing sudden spikes or downturns, quick buying and selling can lead to substantial gains, provided you make informed decisions and act swiftly.

Investing isn't just about numbers; it's an emotional journey, too. Each strategy comes with its psychological aspects. Long-term investing demands patience, sometimes in the face of declining markets. It requires a level of calm and the ability to stick to your plan even when prices take a nosedive. It's about seeing the bigger picture and trusting in the eventual growth of your investments. Short-term trading, on the other hand, requires discipline. The lure of instant profits can lead to impulsive decisions. It's crucial to have a clear strategy and stick to it, avoiding the temptation to chase every promising lead.

For those looking to get the best of both worlds, integrating long-term and short-term tactics can be a viable strategy. The core-satellite approach is one way to achieve this balance. Here, you maintain a core portfolio of long-term investments in stable, reliable cryptocurrencies. This core acts as your foundation, providing stability and growth over time. Around this, you build a satellite of short-term investments, allowing you to capitalize on market volatility and quick gains. This blend offers the security of long-term growth with the excitement of short-term opportunities, creating a diversified and dynamic portfolio.

5.3 REAL-LIFE CASE STUDIES: SUCCESSFUL PORTFOLIO EXAMPLES

Let's dive into some real-world examples of successful cryptocurrency portfolios that have made waves in the market. These aren't just stories of luck but are built on strategic planning, informed decision-making, and calculated risk-taking. First, consider the case of a **high-growth portfolio** that capitalized on the meteoric rise of emerging altcoins while maintaining a solid foundation in established cryptocurrencies. This portfolio included a significant investment in Ethereum and Bitcoin, which served as the bedrock, providing stability and long-term growth potential. Alongside these, the investor allocated funds to promising altcoins like Chainlink and Polkadot, which were poised for rapid growth due to their innovative technologies and strong market positioning.

The success of this portfolio wasn't just about picking the right assets. It was also about understanding market trends and rebalancing the portfolio with precision. The investor actively monitored market conditions, adjusting the allocation of assets in response to new developments and shifting market dynamics. This proactive approach allowed them to capitalize on emerging opportunities while minimizing exposure to declining assets. Rebalancing was done quarterly, ensuring that the portfolio remained aligned with the investor's goals and risk tolerance. This disciplined strategy not only maximized returns but also mitigated risks associated with market volatility and sudden downturns.

Another impressive example is a **balanced risk portfolio** that focused on minimizing exposure to extreme market fluctuations while still achieving steady growth. This portfolio included a mix of stable cryptocurrencies like Bitcoin and Ethereum, complemented by stablecoins such as USD Coin to provide a safety net against market volatility. The investor also explored niche segments within the crypto space, allocating a smaller portion of the portfolio to DeFi tokens and projects with strong fundamentals. The key to this portfolio's success was a meticulous approach to asset selection, prioritizing projects with proven track records, strong development teams, and clear value propositions.

What can we learn from these examples? First, the importance of diversification cannot be overstated. By spreading investments across various assets, these portfolios could mitigate risks and capitalize on growth opportunities in different sectors. Moreover, adaptability to market changes played a crucial role in sustaining success. The ability to adjust strategies and asset allocations in response to evolving market conditions ensured that these portfolios remained resilient and competitive. Another valuable takeaway is the significance of thorough research and due diligence. Successful investors didn't just rely on gut feelings; they conducted in-depth analyses of each asset, considering factors such as technology, market demand, and competitive landscape.

As you reflect on these case studies, consider how the strategies and insights can inform your personal investment approach. Think about the criteria you will use for asset selection and how often you will rebalance your portfolio. Are you prepared to adapt to market changes and seize new opportunities as they arise? Developing a personalized strategy that aligns with your financial goals and risk appetite is essential. By learning from these real-life examples, you can enhance your understanding of what it takes to build a successful cryptocurrency portfolio, equipping yourself with the knowledge and confidence to navigate this dynamic market.

5.4 CRYPTOCURRENCY PORTFOLIO CONSIDERATIONS

Building a cryptocurrency portfolio is like crafting a masterpiece. Every decision adds a brushstroke, contributing to the final picture of your financial aspirations. To guide you through this creative process, here are some questions to consider when constructing your portfolio. These questions build on the discussion in the previous chapter and are designed to help you reflect on your choices, ensuring that your portfolio aligns with your goals and risk tolerance. They serve as a compass, directing your investments and helping you navigate the often turbulent waters of the crypto market.

First, ask yourself about your **investment objectives**.

- What are you hoping to achieve with your cryptocurrency investments?
- Are you looking for long-term wealth accumulation, or are you more interested in short-term gains?

Having clear goals will shape your portfolio structure and guide your decision-making process. Your objectives can determine the balance between stability and risk, influencing which cryptocurrencies you choose and how you allocate your resources.

Next, consider your **risk tolerance**.

- How much volatility are you comfortable with?
- How much can you afford to lose without impacting your financial well-being?

This is crucial, as it will dictate the level of risk you are willing to take on with your investments. A higher risk tolerance might lead you to invest in more volatile assets, while a lower tolerance might steer you towards stablecoins and established cryptocurrencies. Understanding your risk threshold helps you build a portfolio you can manage emotionally and financially.

Think about the amount of **capital** you're willing to invest.

- How much of your total wealth are you prepared to commit to cryptocurrency?

Setting clear boundaries is essential to avoid overcommitting and exposing yourself to unnecessary risk. Determine a percentage of your total assets you feel comfortable investing, ensuring you're not putting your entire financial future on the line. This consideration will help you maintain a balanced and diversified portfolio.

Evaluate the **time frame** you have in mind for your investments.

- Are you planning to hold your assets for years, or do you intend to trade frequently?

Your investment horizon influences the types of assets and strategies you choose. More extended time frames might favor more stable assets that can grow steadily, while shorter time frames might lead you to focus on assets with higher potential for quick gains. Defining your time frame will help you tailor your portfolio to suit your lifestyle and financial goals.

Consider your **knowledge** of the cryptocurrency market.

- How familiar are you with the technologies and projects you're investing in?

Investing in what you understand is essential, as this will give you confidence in your choices and help you make informed decisions. If you're new to the space, start with well-known cryptocurrencies and gradually diversify as you learn more. This approach minimizes risk and allows you to build your expertise alongside your portfolio.

Reflect on your strategy for **staying informed**.

- How will you keep up with market trends and developments?

Staying informed is key to making timely decisions and adjusting your portfolio as needed. To stay updated, consider subscribing to cryptocurrency news platforms, joining online communities, or following industry influencers. Having a reliable source of information ensures you're always aware of market shifts and new opportunities.

Finally, consider your plan for **monitoring and rebalancing your portfolio**.

- How often will you review your investments?
- What criteria will you use to make adjustments?

Regularly assessing your portfolio's performance helps ensure it stays aligned with your goals and risk tolerance. Set a schedule for portfolio reviews and establish guidelines for when and how to rebalance your assets. This proactive approach keeps your investments on track and allows you to capitalize on new opportunities.

With these questions as your guide, you can build a thoughtful and resilient cryptocurrency portfolio. As we wrap up this chapter, remember that your portfolio is an evolving entity, reflecting your financial journey and aspirations. Keep adapting and learning, and you'll find success in the ever-changing world of cryptocurrency. In the next chapter, we'll explore the intricacies of mastering market analysis, diving into strategies to help you make informed decisions and navigate the dynamic crypto landscape.

CHAPTER 6
MASTERING MARKET ANALYSIS

STEP into the world of cryptocurrency, and you'll quickly realize it's not just about buying low and selling high; it's about learning to read the market's mood, behavior, and hidden cues. Like a seasoned traveler who learns to interpret local customs to navigate a foreign city, a successful crypto trader learns to interpret market signals through analysis. This chapter is your guide to understanding those signals, using both technical and fundamental tools to make smarter, more strategic decisions.

At its core, market analysis is about recognizing patterns, evaluating data, and anticipating change. It helps you answer questions like: *Is this price trend sustainable? Are traders optimistic or fearful? Is this project fundamentally sound, or is it just hype?* Whether you're looking at historical price charts or diving into a project's financial health, market analysis is the compass that helps you navigate the often chaotic seas of crypto trading.

We'll begin with **technical analysis**, which focuses on price movements, chart patterns, and indicators like RSI, MACD, and Bollinger Bands. These tools don't just show you what *has* happened; they help you predict what *might* happen next by interpreting visual cues and momentum shifts in the market.

Next, we'll explore **fundamental analysis**, which takes a step back from the charts and digs into the core of a cryptocurrency project – its economic foundation, utility, team, partnerships, and how external factors like regulations or global news shape market sentiment.

6.1 TECHNICAL ANALYSIS: CHARTS, PATTERNS, AND TECHNICAL INDICATORS

Technical analysis in crypto focuses on price charts, patterns, and indicators (like RSI, MACD, or Bollinger Bands) to predict future market movements. It's based on the idea that historical price behavior can help forecast future trends, without considering the asset's underlying value. To begin our journey into technical analysis, we'll start with one of the most iconic and widely used tools in a trader's arsenal: the **candlestick chart**. Far more than just a visual display of numbers, candlestick charts offer a rich, intuitive way to interpret price behavior, revealing the mood of the market at a glance.

Imagine you're an art collector standing before a painting. Each brushstroke, each color, tells a story and holds a clue to the artist's intent. Similarly, candlestick charts are the canvases of cryptocurrency markets, offering visual insights into price movements and trader sentiments. Originating in Japan over a century ago, these charts have become essential tools for traders worldwide. They don't just show data; they narrate the emotional journey of the market, highlighting short-term trends and potential reversals. They display historical price data, capturing the open, close, high, and low prices for any given period in a visually intuitive way. The body of the candlestick represents the range between the opening and closing prices, while the shadows, or wicks, mark the highs and lows. A filled body, often red or black, signifies a close lower than the open, suggesting bearish sentiment. In contrast, a hollow body, in green or white, signals bullish behavior when the close is higher than the open.

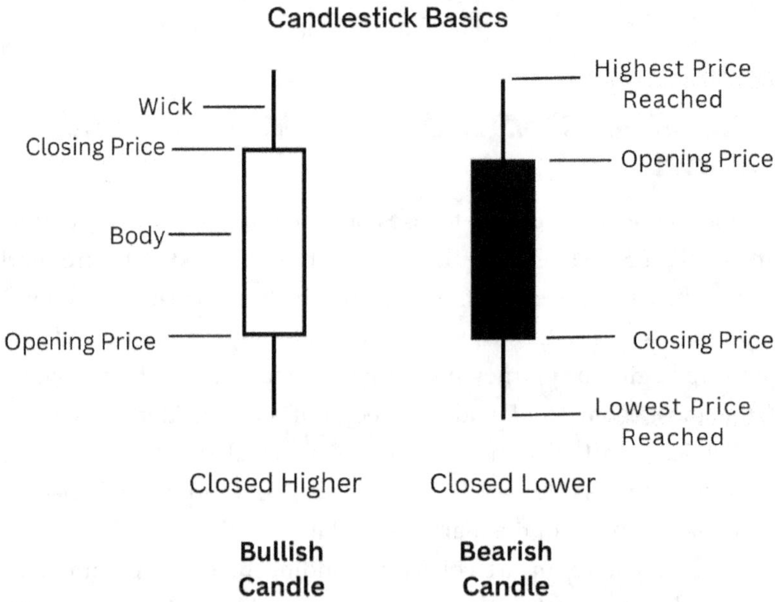

To truly harness the power of candlestick charts, you must dive into their patterns. These patterns are like the language of the market, with each formation carrying specific implications. Take the **bullish engulfing pattern**, for instance. It appears when a small, bearish candle is followed by a larger, bullish candle that completely engulfs the previous one. This pattern often signals a potential upward reversal, indicating that buyers have taken control. On the other hand, the **bearish engulfing pattern** shows a small bullish candle engulfed by a larger bearish one, hinting at a downward shift as sellers gain the upper hand.

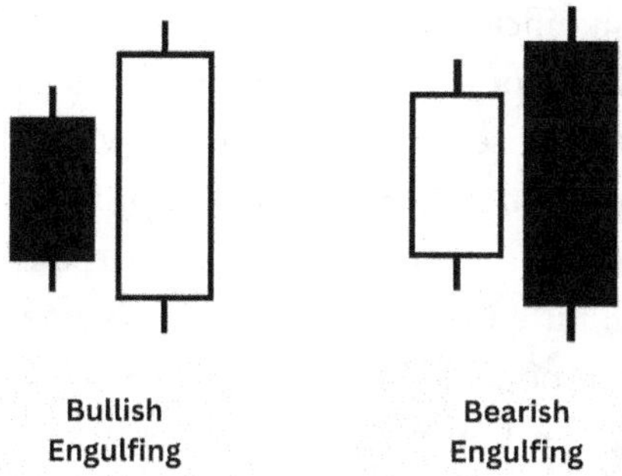

Then there's the **doji**, a unique candlestick that forms when the open and close prices are virtually identical, creating a cross or plus sign. It suggests indecision in the market and can signal a potential reversal in market direction, especially if found at the top or bottom of a trend, making it a critical moment for traders to pay attention to. There are different types of doji patterns, such as the gravestone doji (often seen as a bearish reversal) and the dragonfly doji (often seen as a bullish reversal).

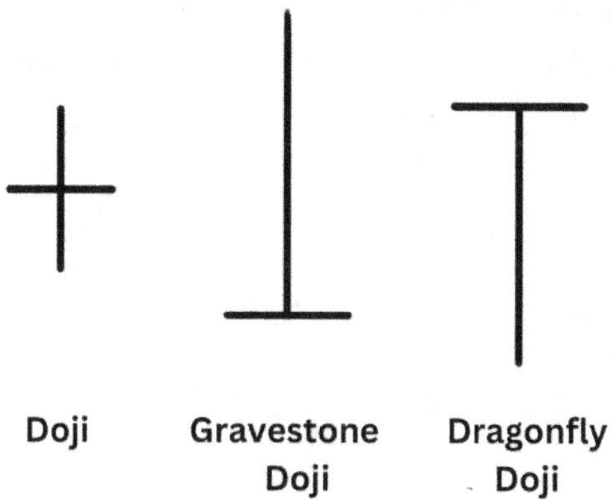

There are many candlestick patterns that can be used for analysis purposes. As you become more confident and experienced in performing analyses, it's important to familiarize yourself with these patterns. You can find many resources online that explain the different patterns and their significance.

Timeframes add another layer of depth to candlestick charts, offering you different lenses through which to view the market. Short-term trends are captured in intraday charts, providing granularity for day traders who thrive on quick decisions. These charts might show hourly or even minute-by-minute price movements, allowing for precise entry and exit points. However, they can be volatile, with rapid shifts that demand constant attention. In contrast, daily charts high-light long-term trends, smoothing out the noise and providing a broader perspective. They cater to swing traders and long-term investors who seek to ride more sustained trends. These varying time frames allow you to tailor your analysis to your trading style, whether you prefer the fast-paced world of intraday trading or the steady insights of daily charts.

Candlestick patterns are invaluable in decision-making, serving as signposts that guide traders toward strategic moves. By interpreting these patterns, traders can identify entry and exit points, maximizing profits and minimizing losses. For instance, spotting a bullish engulfing pattern might tempt you to enter a long position, antici-pating upward momentum. Conversely, a bearish engulfing pattern could signal an exit, protecting your gains before a potential decline. These patterns also help identify market trend reversals, alerting you to shifts before they fully unfold.

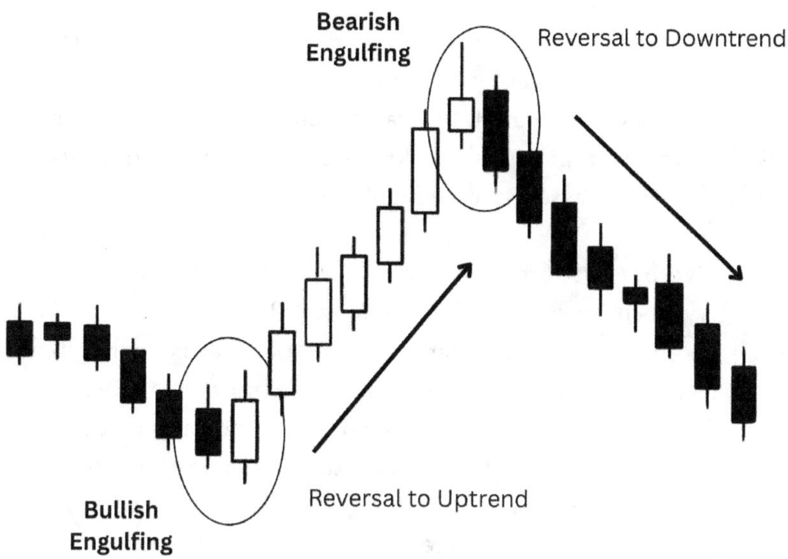

Candlestick charts are invaluable for examining price shifts, gauging market mood, and spotting potential reversals in trends. However, their true power is unlocked when paired with other technical analysis tools. We'll discuss some of them in the following section, and others you should become familiar with after you master the basics. Some of the more popular tools include:

- Relative Strength Index (RSI)
- Moving Averages
- Moving Average Convergence Divergence (MACD)
- Bollinger Bands
- Fibonacci Retracement Levels
- Ichimoku Cloud

Combining these tools with candlestick charts allows for a deeper analysis of patterns and trends, offering clearer insights into where prices might head in the future.

Relative Strength Index (RSI)

The RSI is a valuable tool for assessing the mood of the cryptocurrency market. It acts like a market thermometer, indicating whether an asset is overheating or cooling off. RSI values range from 0 to 100, calculated based on the average gains and losses over a designated period, and signal whether an asset is overbought or oversold.

- **Overbought**: If the RSI score is above 70, it suggests that the cryptocurrency might be overbought. This means many people have been buying it, and its price may be higher than its typical value, which could lead to a price drop soon.
- **Oversold**: If the RSI score is below 30, it indicates that the cryptocurrency might be oversold. This suggests that the price has fallen sharply, and it might be undervalued, which could lead to a price increase as buyers start to see it as a good deal.

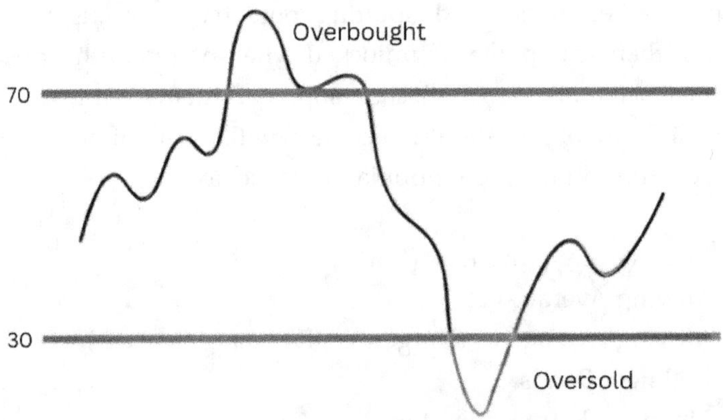

For a more detailed analysis, you can combine RSI with a candlestick chart. When you look at a candlestick chart, you can see patterns that suggest future movements in price. By using the RSI, you can validate these patterns. For example, if a candlestick pattern suggests an upcoming reversal and the RSI indicates the asset is either overbought or oversold, it strengthens the case for that reversal.

This combination allows you to make more informed decisions by confirming signals from both tools. If both the candlestick pattern and the RSI point towards a potential increase in price, it might be a good time to consider buying. Conversely, if both suggest a decrease, it might be time to sell.

Moving Average Convergence Divergence (MACD)

Another powerful tool in your trading toolkit is the Moving Average Convergence Divergence (MACD). A **moving average** is used to determine the trend direction and is calculated by adding up all the data points over a specific period and dividing by the sum of the number of periods. The **MACD** helps to identify momentum shifts to determine if the price of an asset is strengthening or weakening and helps to spot potential buy or sell signals. Picture two lines dancing on a chart: the MACD line and the signal line. When the MACD line crosses above the signal line, it might be time to consider buying, as this crossover indicates bullish momentum. Conversely, when it dips below, bearish sentiment takes the stage, signaling a potential sell. The histogram, a series of vertical bars, adds another layer of insight by showing the distance between these two lines. Positive bars suggest strengthening momentum, while negative ones point to potential weakness. Divergences in MACD can also be telling. If the price hits a new high while MACD doesn't, it might be a warning that the trend is losing steam.

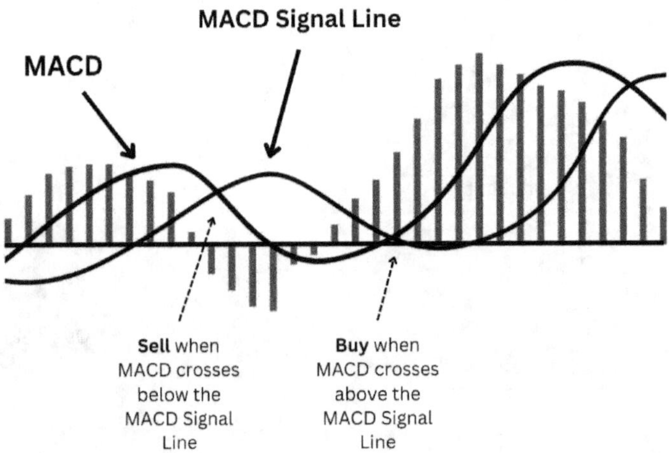

Bollinger Bands

Bollinger Bands are a technical indicator that gives you a sense of the market's volatility and trend direction. Developed by John Bollinger, this indicator tool consists of three bands. The middle band is the simple moving average (typically a 20-day average), and the two outer bands reflect standard deviations. The top one is the average plus two standard deviations, and the lower is the average minus two standard deviations. The standard deviation is a measure of how much the price deviates from the average over a given period and is an indication of volatility. The bands being farther apart indicate higher volatility, and closer bands indicate lower volatility. When the price touches the upper band, it signals potential overbought conditions, while reaching the lower band suggests oversold levels. The bands expand and contract based on market volatility. A squeeze, where the bands come closer, hints at a potential breakout, while a wide band spread often indicates high volatility. The key lies in recognizing these movements as opportunities. For instance, a Bollinger Band squeeze followed by a breakout might signal the start of a new trend.

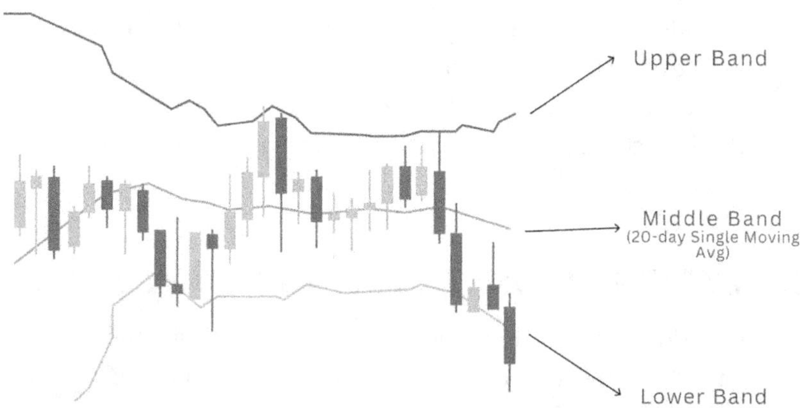

Using RSI, MACD, and Bollinger Bands together can provide a comprehensive view of market dynamics. Imagine you're analyzing a cryptocurrency and notice that RSI indicates an overbought condition. At the same time, the MACD shows a bearish crossover (the MACD line crosses below the signal line). This double confirmation might suggest it's time to consider selling. Conversely, if Bollinger Bands show a squeeze and RSI is in the oversold territory while MACD begins forming a bullish crossover (MACD crosses above the signal line), these combined signals could point to a ripe buying opportunity. By layering these indicators, you gain a multi-dimensional perspective, helping you make informed decisions that align with your strategy.

Charting Platforms

There are resources available online to help with technical analysis. These platforms provide interactive charts and access to indicators, patterns, and drawing tools:

- **TradingView** – The most popular charting tool for crypto and other asset classes. Offers real-time charts and indicators.
- **CryptoCompare** – Offers both price tracking and basic charting tools.
- **Coinigy** – All-in-one crypto trading platform with charting and exchange integration.
- **Binance, Coinbase Pro, Kraken** – Many exchanges have built-in charting tools powered by TradingView or similar platforms.

6.2 FUNDAMENTAL ANALYSIS: ECONOMIC AND FINANCIAL FACTORS

In the world of cryptocurrency, fundamental analysis goes beyond charts and patterns to explore the broader economic and financial forces that drive market behavior. This type of analysis evaluates a project's underlying value and long-term potential, taking into account factors such as economic indicators, financial stability, technological innovation, and market sentiment.

A key component of this approach is **financial analysis**, which helps distinguish between well-funded, sustainable projects and those that may struggle to survive once market hype fades. While not every crypto project provides complete transparency, taking the time to explore available financial data gives you a strategic edge and helps identify assets with real staying power. Strong projects often disclose how they allocate resources, maintain sustainable spending, and generate income through real utility, such as transaction fees or staking.

Unlike traditional assets, crypto prices are heavily influenced by a combination of tangible data and intangible sentiment. **Economic indicators** such as inflation, interest rates, or employment figures can influence investor behavior, just as they do in traditional financial markets. However, in crypto, investor sentiment often plays an even larger role. Market confidence can drive prices sharply upward, while fear and uncertainty can trigger rapid sell-offs.

News and events frequently act as catalysts for these sentiment-driven swings. Regulatory developments, in particular, tend to have a significant impact. Announcements of tighter restrictions can spark concern over compliance burdens or trading limitations, leading to price drops. On the other hand, positive regulatory news can reassure investors, boosting market confidence and asset values.

Technological advancements can lead to price surges as investor interest increases. Breakthroughs, such as improved security features, scalable blockchain solutions, or partnerships with major companies, often capture headlines and attract new investors. These developments enhance a cryptocurrency's perceived utility and credibility, leading to increased demand and upward price movement.

Incorporating news analysis into your trading strategy involves more than just reacting to headlines. It's important to evaluate the credibility of news sources, prioritizing established financial publications while cross-referencing multiple outlets to verify the accuracy of claims. Not all news carries equal weight, so understanding the historical market impact of similar announcements can help you better anticipate likely outcomes. For example, if previous regulatory crackdowns led to sharp declines, similar news in the future may prompt a comparable reaction.

By integrating this type of analysis, traders can make more informed decisions and adjust their strategies proactively. Expecting a favorable regulatory shift? Consider entering a position early. Worried about negative press or uncertain government policy? It may be wise to reduce exposure. While news analysis doesn't guarantee predictions, it enables you to stay ahead of developments and respond with agility – an essential skill in a market as dynamic and volatile as cryptocurrency.

6.3 APPLYING ANALYSIS IN REAL-LIFE SCENARIOS

Imagine you're at a sports game, and the crowd roars as the underdog suddenly scores, shifting the momentum of the match. Like in sports, the cryptocurrency market is full of moments where shifts happen, often driven by unexpected news or trends. Take, for instance, the significant price surge of Bitcoin that occurred when the first Bitcoin ETF received approval. This wasn't just a random spike; it was a result of strategic foresight by savvy traders who anticipated the impact of the approval. By analyzing market sentiment and regulatory developments, these traders positioned themselves ahead of time, buying Bitcoin before the official announcement. This proactive approach allowed them to capitalize on the subsequent price jump, showcasing the power of combining technical and fundamental analysis in real-world scenarios.

In another example, consider the case of an altcoin rally triggered by a major partnership announcement. Imagine a lesser-known cryptocurrency suddenly gaining traction due to a collaboration with a leading tech company. Traders who diligently follow industry news might have caught wind of initial partnership talks and started accumulating the altcoin early. As the partnership was confirmed and widely publicized, a surge in buying interest drove the altcoin's price higher, rewarding those who anticipated the market's reaction. In both cases, the key was not just reacting to news but predicting its impact and acting strategically in advance.

For traders to effectively apply analysis, it's crucial to break down the decision-making process systematically. Setting up entry and exit points is a foundational step. Before entering a trade, determine your target entry point based on technical indicators and market trends. Equally important is identifying a suitable exit strategy, whether to secure profits or cut losses. This step requires discipline and adherence to your predetermined plan, avoiding impulsive decisions driven by market fluctuations. Risk management is another critical consideration. Define how much of your portfolio you're willing to risk on a single trade and set stop-loss orders to limit potential losses. By assessing risk and reward ratios, you ensure that your trades align with your overall strategy and risk tolerance.

Market analysis is not without its challenges and limitations. Analyzing conflicting signals can be frustrating, as indicators may present mixed messages that cloud decision-making. Prioritizing key indicators and maintaining a clear focus on your chosen strategy is essential. Sudden market reversals are another hurdle. Crypto markets are notorious for their volatility, and unexpected shifts can disrupt even the most well-researched trades. Flexibility and adaptability are key in such situations, allowing you to reassess your strategy and pivot when necessary.

Continuous practice and adaptation are the cornerstones of successful market analysis. Regularly backtesting your strategies against historical data can provide valuable insights into their effectiveness. By analyzing past trades, you identify strengths and weaknesses, enabling you to refine your approach. Staying up to date with market trends is equally important. Cryptocurrency markets evolve rapidly, with new developments constantly shaping the landscape. By staying up to date with the latest news and technological advancements, you position yourself to make informed decisions and capitalize on emerging opportunities.

In closing, real-life scenarios highlight the dynamic nature of cryptocurrency trading. The ability to anticipate market shifts, set strategic entry and exit points, and adapt to challenges is essential. As you continue to engage with the market, remember that each trade is an opportunity to learn and grow. Your journey is unique, and by embracing ongoing learning and flexibility, you'll navigate the complexities of the crypto world with confidence. As we transition to the next chapter, we'll dive deeper into managing risks and protecting your investments, ensuring you're equipped for whatever the market throws your way.

CHAPTER 7
EFFECTIVE RISK MANAGEMENT

PICTURE THIS: You're walking a tightrope suspended high in the air. Every step calls for focus, balance, and calculated movement. Navigating the world of cryptocurrency trading is much the same – managing risk requires discipline and a well-thought-out strategy to stay steady amid the market's unpredictable twists and turns. One of the most valuable tools at your disposal to manage risk is the stop-loss order. It's a safety net that can prevent a minor slip from turning into a disastrous fall. Let's delve into how this tool can serve as your safety harness in the volatile world of crypto.

Stop-loss orders are your automatic sell triggers, designed to limit potential losses by setting predetermined exit points. Think of them as an insurance policy for your investments. When the market price hits a specific trigger price that you set, the stop-loss order automatically kicks into action, closing the position to prevent further losses. This can be especially helpful in volatile markets, where prices can plummet with little warning. By establishing a stop-loss, you're essentially saying, "If this ship starts sinking, I'll be the first in the lifeboat." It's a proactive measure that ensures you're not caught off-guard, providing a layer of protection against significant financial setbacks.

Determining the right stop-loss levels are crucial to making this strategy work for you. It's about finding that sweet spot where you can protect your investment without stifling your potential gains. One common method is using percentage-based stop-losses. For instance, you might set a stop-loss to activate if your asset falls by 10% from its purchase price. This approach is straightforward and easy to implement, especially for beginners. Alternatively, you can base your stop-loss on support and resistance levels, which are key price points that an asset struggles to go below (support) or above (resistance). By setting your stop-loss just below a support level, you can avoid selling prematurely during a temporary price dip.

Like any tool, stop-loss orders come with their pros and cons. On the plus side, they help you avoid emotional panic sells, where fear of loss might otherwise push you to make hasty decisions. They allow you to stay calm and collected, knowing that a plan is in place. However, a downside to be aware of is the risk of triggering a stop-loss during a temporary market dip. Markets can be unpredictable, and a brief dip might trigger your stop-loss, only for the price to rebound shortly after. It's like an overcautious alarm system that goes off at the slightest hint of smoke, even when there's no fire. Being mindful of these nuances can help you set more effective stop-loss points.

Consider the scenario of a trader who sets a **trailing stop-loss** to protect gains. A trailing stop-loss moves with the market price, maintaining a set percentage below the peak price achieved since the position was opened. This means if the price rises, the stop-loss adjusts upward, locking in profits while still allowing for potential gains. Conversely, a **fixed stop-loss** might be more suitable for high-risk assets where volatility is expected. By setting a firm limit on potential losses, you can engage in high-stakes trades with a safety net in place, knowing exactly where your exit point lies.

7.1 DIVERSIFICATION STRATEGIES TO MINIMIZE RISK

Diversification is a fundamental strategy in risk management, particularly in the volatile world of cryptocurrency investing. Unlike traditional markets, cryptocurrencies can exhibit extreme price swings that can lead to significant gains or losses within a short period. To mitigate such risks, diversification across various cryptocurrencies can be a prudent strategy and involves spreading your investment across different types of assets within the crypto space. This can include major cryptocurrencies like Bitcoin and Ethereum, which are generally more stable due to their larger market caps and broader adoption. However, it also involves investing in smaller altcoins and possibly even tokens associated with specific projects or industries. Each category of crypto asset behaves differently depending on market conditions, technological developments, and regulatory news, thus balancing the portfolio's performance over time.

Moreover, diversification isn't just about selecting different currencies; it also includes considering different sectors within the crypto industry, such as finance (DeFi), supply chain (logistics), and arts (NFTs). This sectoral diversification ensures that an investor's portfolio isn't overly dependent on the success or failure of a single sector within the crypto economy. For example, while DeFi might be thriving, other sectors like NFTs could be facing a downturn, and having investments in both areas could balance out the overall portfolio performance. These sectors offer unique opportunities and can provide exposure to different growth trends within the crypto industry.

Understanding these dynamics is crucial, especially when considering mechanisms for risk management, such as the use of stablecoins. Stablecoins are particularly valuable in risk management and can hedge against volatility. They offer a way to park your investments during periods of high market turbulence without exiting the crypto market entirely. For instance, if you anticipate a market downturn, moving a portion of your holdings into stablecoins can preserve your portfolio's value until conditions improve. This approach reduces your exposure to market swings, allowing you to re-enter the market when you're more confident in the direction of asset prices.

Diversification offers numerous benefits. It can significantly reduce volatility, smoothing out the roller coaster ride that investing often feels like. However, it's not without its challenges. One potential pitfall is over-diversification, where you spread your investments too thin. This can dilute your returns, as you might end up with a vast array of assets that are difficult to manage and track. The complexity of managing diverse assets can become overwhelming, especially for beginners. It's crucial to strike a balance between diversification and focus, ensuring that you have a manageable number of investments that you can actively monitor and understand. This balance allows you to reap the benefits of diversification without becoming bogged down in complexity.

7.2 STRATEGIES TO AVOID EMOTIONAL TRADING DECISIONS

Trading cryptocurrencies can be an emotional rollercoaster. Market volatility often triggers fear and greed, leading to decisions that aren't always rational. Imagine watching your investment's value plummet within minutes. Panic sets in, urging you to sell before the losses deepen. This fear-driven reaction is common in traders facing volatile markets. On the flip side, there's FOMO (Fear of Missing Out) which creeps in as you see a rising asset and worry about missing the opportunity to profit. Both scenarios tug at your emotions, potentially leading you down a path of hasty choices rather than calculated decisions.

Emotions, powerful as they are, can significantly impact trading outcomes. When fear takes the wheel, you might find yourself panic selling during market downturns, locking in losses that could have been avoided if you were patient and waited it out. Conversely, greed can drive you to chase losses, doubling down on investments in hopes of a quick recovery. This impulsive behavior can spiral into a cycle of poor decisions, increasing risk and diminishing returns. Emotional trading often clouds judgment, steering you away from your strategy and into the unpredictable waters of speculation. Recognizing these emotional triggers is the first step toward maintaining control.

Maintaining emotional control in trading is no small feat, but there are strategies to keep your cool. Start by developing a trading journal. Documenting your trades, thoughts, and emotions can provide clarity, helping you spot patterns in your decision-making process. This self-awareness is vital in understanding when emotions are influencing your choices. Mindfulness and stress management practices, such as meditation or deep breathing exercises, can also help you stay centered, reducing the impact of anxiety and fear. Consider setting predefined rules for your trades. These rules act as a safeguard, guiding your actions even when emotions threaten to take over. By sticking to these rules, you rely on logic rather than impulse, making decisions based on strategy rather than emotion.

Many traders have walked this path and emerged victorious by mastering emotional control. Take, for instance, the story of a trader who initially struggled with knee-jerk reactions to market shifts. By incorporating a trading journal and mindfulness techniques, they transformed their approach, achieving consistency in their result, and learned the power of discipline and self-awareness in trading. Learning from those who've successfully navigated emotional challenges can be inspiring and enlightening. It shows that emotional control is attainable with dedication and the proper techniques.

The trading journey is as much about understanding markets as it is about understanding yourself. By identifying emotional triggers and implementing strategies to manage them, you can trade with clarity and confidence. Remember, emotions are a natural part of trading, but they don't have to dictate your decisions. With practice and persistence, you can train yourself to recognize emotional cues and respond with a level-headed approach. Trading is an area where logic should always prevail over emotion, and mastering this balance can lead to greater success and satisfaction in your trading endeavors.

7.3 LEARNING FROM LOSSES: TURNING MISTAKES INTO LESSONS

In cryptocurrency trading, losses are as inevitable as the sun rising. While the excitement of gains often takes center stage, the reality is that every trader, no matter how seasoned, faces downturns. The key lies not in avoiding these losses altogether but in learning from them. Consider the learning curve in trading as similar to mastering any new skill – it takes time, patience, and a willingness to stumble, fall, and get back up. Embracing a growth mindset in the face of setbacks can be transformative. Instead of viewing a loss as a failure, see it as a stepping stone – a chance to learn and refine your strategies. This shift in perspective can turn losses into valuable lessons that pave the way for future successes.

Reflecting on and analyzing your losses is a practice that can lead to profound insights. After a trade that didn't go as planned, take time to dissect what happened. Was it a misjudgment of market trends or perhaps an emotional decision made in the heat of the moment? Post-trade analysis is crucial here. By examining the details of each trade, you can identify patterns and mistakes that might have gone unnoticed. Look for recurring themes: Are you consistently buying at the wrong time or selling too early? Recognizing these patterns can help you adjust your approach and avoid similar pitfalls in the future. This constructive reflection turns trading losses into a powerful learning tool, building a foundation for improved performance.

Adopting a resilient mindset is vital in the trading world. It's about bouncing back from setbacks with renewed determination. Embracing failure as an integral part of success can liberate you from the fear of making mistakes. Each loss becomes a lesson, a chance to grow stronger and wiser. Building mental toughness allows you to withstand the ups and downs of trading without losing your confidence. It's about developing the ability to adapt to changing circumstances and persist even when the going gets tough. This resilience separates successful traders from those who may give up at the first sign of trouble. It's a quality that can be cultivated over time through experience, reflection, and a commitment to continuous improvement.

Let's turn to the stories of traders who faced significant losses yet managed to turn their fortunes around. Take, for example, a trader who found themselves on the brink of giving up after a series of bad trades. Instead of walking away, they chose to analyze their missteps, identify weaknesses in their strategy, and make necessary adjustments. Through perseverance and a willingness to learn, they eventually achieved consistent success. Such comeback stories are not uncommon. Public trading figures often share their journeys, highlighting the importance of resilience and learning from setbacks. These narratives serve as powerful reminders that success in trading isn't about avoiding losses but using them as stepping stones toward greater achievements.

7.4 RISK MANAGEMENT QUIZ: TEST YOUR KNOWLEDGE

So, you've taken in a lot about risk management in cryptocurrency. Now it's time to see how much you've absorbed. This quiz will help cement your understanding and pinpoint areas you might want to revisit. It's designed to be insightful, not intimidating, so take a deep breath and let's get started.

True or False

1. A stop-loss order guarantees that your position will be closed at the price you set, even in a highly volatile market. (True/False)
2. Diversification eliminates all investment risk. (True/False)
3. Keeping a trading journal can help manage emotions by providing a record of past decisions and their outcomes. (True/False)

Multiple Choice

4. What does a stop-loss order do if the market takes a nosedive and you're not at your computer?
   - A) It buys more of the asset
   - B) It sells the asset at a predetermined price
   - C) It sends you an alert to check the market
5. Which of the following strategies best describes diversification?
   - A) Investing only in Bitcoin
   - B) Spreading investments across multiple cryptocurrencies
   - C) Holding only stablecoins

4. What's a common emotional trigger that can lead to impulsive trades?
    - A) Following a well-researched plan
    - B) Fear of Missing Out (FOMO) on a rising asset
    - C) Setting predefined rules

Answers & Explanations

1. False
    - Explanation: Stop-loss orders aim to limit losses but do not guarantee the exact exit price in volatile markets due to slippage (the difference in the price between the time the order is placed and when it is filled).
2. False
    - Explanation: Diversification reduces risk but does not eliminate it completely. It's a way to manage risk, not remove it.
3. True
    - Explanation: A trading journal helps identify emotional patterns and improve decision-making through self-reflection.
4. B) It sells the asset at a predetermined price
    - Explanation: Stop-loss orders automatically sell your asset when it hits a specific price, helping to limit your losses.
5. B) Spreading investments across multiple cryptocurrencies
    - Explanation: Diversification means investing in a variety of assets to reduce risk exposure.
6. B) Fear of Missing Out (FOMO) on a rising asset
    - Explanation: FOMO often causes traders to make impulsive decisions that stray from their planned strategy.

Final Thoughts

As you navigate the thrilling yet unpredictable world of cryptocurrency, mastering risk management becomes your steady guide. From stop-loss orders to diversification and keeping emotions in check, each strategy holds the key to wiser investment decisions. With a solid understanding of these concepts, you're better prepared to make informed choices that align with your financial goals.

Remember, the cryptocurrency market is ever-evolving, and staying agile and informed is essential. In the next chapter, we'll delve deeper into the intricacies of entry and exit strategies, equipping you with the knowledge to time your trades effectively and maximize your potential for success. Let's continue building on this foundation.

CHAPTER 8

ENTRY AND EXIT STRATEGIES

PICTURE A SURFER WAITING for the perfect wave. They study the ocean's rhythm, patiently anticipating the moment to paddle and ride the swell to shore. Identifying the right entry point in cryptocurrency trading is like catching that wave. Timing is critical, as entering a trade at the right moment can significantly impact your potential gains. Jumping in too early might leave you paddling aimlessly, while waiting too long could mean missing the wave entirely. By honing your skills in recognizing optimal entry points, you set yourself up for success in the ever-changing seas of cryptocurrency.

The importance of timing your entry cannot be overstated. Just as buying a car right before a new model release might result in overpaying, purchasing cryptocurrency at its peak can lead to disappointment as prices drop. The goal is to avoid these peaks by leveraging market trends and entering when prices have room to grow. This requires a keen sense of the market's pulse and an understanding of when to wait and when to act. By mastering this art, you position yourself to capitalize on price upswings, maximizing your potential profits.

Technical indicators are invaluable tools to aid in identifying strategic entry points. Moving averages, for instance, provide a smoothed-out view of price trends over time, helping you spot when a trend may be reversing or gaining strength. A moving average crossover occurs when a short-term moving average crosses above a long-term average, suggesting potential upward momentum. Meanwhile, Fibonacci retracement levels are like roadmaps, marking potential support and resistance levels based on the mathematical Fibonacci sequence. These levels often coincide with points where traders expect a price to reverse, offering clues to optimal entry opportunities.

Support and resistance levels are the foundation of any strong entry strategy. Support is like a safety net – the level where prices often stop falling and begin to rise again. On the other hand, resistance acts like a ceiling, where upward momentum tends to stall, and prices may reverse. When the price nears a support level, it can signal a potential bounce, making it an opportune moment to consider buying. Conversely, when the price approaches resistance, it might hint at a reversal or, in some cases, a breakout to new highs. Recognizing these zones allows you to time your entries with greater confidence and precision.

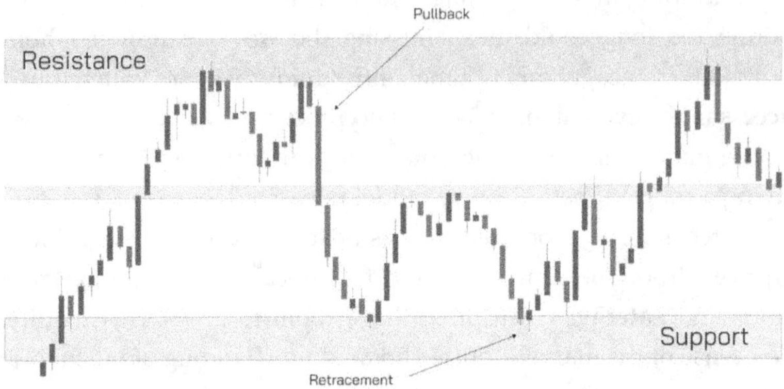

Consider the scenario of market consolidation, where prices are moving within a narrow range, neither rising nor falling significantly. This can be an ideal time to enter a trade, as it often precedes a breakout where prices move sharply in one direction. Another strategy is to wait for a trend reversal confirmation. Imagine a downtrend where prices have been consistently dropping. Using moving averages and support levels, you might identify a point where the trend shows signs of reversing. Entering after this confirmation can position you to ride the wave of a new upward trend.

8.1 SETTING PROFITABLE EXIT STRATEGIES

Think of exit strategies as the unsung heroes in your trading toolkit. They're behind the scenes, ensuring your profits are locked in and your losses are limited. While riding the highs of a trade is thrilling, knowing when to step off the roller coaster is equally crucial. A well-planned exit strategy helps you avoid rash decisions driven by emotion. Instead of getting swept up in the excitement or panic of market fluctuations, you have a clear plan guiding your next moves. This clarity protects your gains from unexpected market reversals, allowing you to breathe easy knowing you've secured your earnings.

Technical indicators are valuable tools to determine when to exit a trade. The Relative Strength Index (RSI) is a popular tool that signals when an asset might be overbought, suggesting it's time to consider selling. On the other hand, the Moving Average Convergence Divergence (MACD) helps you spot momentum shifts. By analyzing the relationship between two moving averages of an asset's price, the MACD offers clues about changes in momentum, which can guide your exit decisions.

Trailing stop-loss orders are another powerful tool in your arsenal. Unlike fixed stop-losses that remain static, trailing stop-losses move with the market, adjusting as prices rise. This dynamic feature allows you to protect your profits without prematurely exiting a trade. When the market moves in your favor, the trailing stop-loss follows along, maintaining a set distance below the market price. If the market reverses direction, the trailing stop-loss kicks in, securing your gains before they evaporate. In volatile markets, this adaptability can be the difference between a profitable trade and a missed opportunity.

Consider a scenario where a trader enters a position as an asset approaches a resistance level. As the price climbs and nears this level, the trader sets a trailing stop-loss to lock in gains. If the price continues to rise, the trailing stop-loss follows, ensuring profits are captured. However, if the price hits the resistance and reverses, the stop-loss activates, protecting the trader from further losses. Another effective exit strategy involves selling during bullish exhaustion. When an asset has experienced a prolonged upward trend, signs of exhaustion may appear, such as decreasing volume or bearish candlestick patterns. Recognizing these signals and exiting before the trend reverses helps preserve profits and minimizes exposure to downturns.

As you gain experience trading, a helpful way to reinforce your understanding of exit strategies is to reflect on past trades. Consider times when you successfully exited a trade and the factors that influenced your decision. Was there a specific indicator or market condition that guided you? Conversely, think about trades where an exit strategy could have improved your outcome. By analyzing these experiences, you can refine your approach and increase your confidence in setting profitable exits. Remember that exit strategies are not just about maximizing profits but also about managing risk and maintaining control over your trading activities.

8.2 TIMING THE MARKET: MYTHS VS. REALITY

In the world of cryptocurrency trading, there's a tantalizing allure to the idea of timing the market perfectly. It's the dream of buying low and selling high, striking just at the right moment to maximize profits. But let's clear the air – this notion of perfect timing is essentially a myth. The belief that one can consistently predict market movements with pinpoint accuracy is a misconception often fueled by hindsight bias. Remember, markets are inherently unpredictable, influenced by countless factors ranging from economic shifts to geopolitical events. Even seasoned traders, with years of experience and knowledge under their belts, often find themselves caught off guard by unexpected market turns.

Trying to time the market perfectly isn't just challenging; it's downright stressful. The constant pressure to predict the next move can lead to psychological stress, decision fatigue, and even burnout. For many, the emotional rollercoaster of wins and losses becomes overwhelming, clouding judgment and leading to impulsive decisions. In addition, external events – like regulatory changes or global crises – can impact market movements in ways that are difficult to foresee. These factors make it clear that attempting to time the market can often result in buying high and selling low, the opposite of what traders aspire to achieve.

Given the challenges, many traders turn to alternative strategies focusing on long-term success rather than short-term timing. One popular approach is **dollar-cost averaging**, where you invest a fixed amount at regular intervals, regardless of the market's ups and downs. This method reduces the impact of market volatility and helps mitigate the risks associated with trying to time entry points perfectly. Another strategy is **value investing**, which involves buying assets that are undervalued by the market and holding them until their intrinsic value is recognized. This approach is less about timing and more about understanding an asset's long-term potential. **Trend-following techniques**, where traders ride existing market trends rather than anticipating reversals, also offer a way to align with market momentum without the need for perfect timing.

Listening to experienced traders can provide valuable insights into navigating the complexities of market timing. Many seasoned traders emphasize the importance of patience, discipline, and maintaining a long-term perspective. Learning from market missteps is another key lesson. Traders who've experienced significant losses often point to the dangers of relying solely on timing strategies, advocating for diversified portfolios and sound risk management practices instead.

Ultimately, the reality of market timing is that it's more art than science, filled with challenges and uncertainties. Trying to predict every market twist and turn can lead to frustration and losses. By focusing on proven strategies like dollar-cost averaging and value investing – alongside insights from those who've navigated these waters – you can shift your focus from the elusive pursuit of perfect timing to the attainable goal of long-term success.

8.3 ADAPTING STRATEGIES TO MARKET CHANGES

In the dynamic world of cryptocurrency trading, flexibility and adaptability are your best allies. Imagine trying to navigate a fast-moving river; standing rigidly will only lead to being swept away. Instead, you must be responsive, adjusting your stance with each twist and turn. This is how traders should approach changing market conditions. The crypto landscape is notorious for its volatility, with prices influenced by many factors. As a trader, the ability to pivot and modify your strategies in response to these changes can be the difference between success and failure.

Assessing market conditions involves more than just glancing at price charts. It requires a comprehensive understanding of various macroeconomic indicators and how they influence cryptocurrency markets. For instance, changes in interest rates, inflation data, or geopolitical events can affect investor sentiment and market dynamics. By closely monitoring these indicators, you can better predict potential market shifts and adjust your trading strategies accordingly. Evaluating market sentiment is equally important. Sentiment can be gauged through news outlets, social media chatter, and even the tone of public statements from influential figures. A rise in positive sentiment might indicate a bullish market, while negative sentiment could signal impending downturns.

Several techniques can be employed to refine and align your strategies with current market dynamics. One effective method is **backtesting**, where you apply your strategy to historical data to see how it would have performed. This lets you tweak and optimize your approach based on real-world scenarios without risking actual capital. Incorporating **feedback loops** is another valuable technique. You create a continuous improvement cycle by consistently reviewing your trades and outcomes and learning from successes and failures. **Iterative strategy development** is about making incremental adjustments to your trading plan, testing each change's impact, and refining your approach in a structured manner. This adaptability ensures your strategies remain relevant and effective in an ever-evolving market.

There are numerous stories of traders who have successfully adapted their strategies to thrive amidst market changes. Take the case of a trader who managed to pivot during a bearish market. Initially, they focused on long positions but quickly realized the market was turning south. By analyzing macroeconomic indicators and sentiment, they shifted to short positions and hedged their investments, minimizing losses and even turning a profit. Another example involves a trader who adjusted their strategies in response to new regulations. When a country announced strict crypto regulations, this trader diversified their portfolio, investing in assets less affected by the regulatory environment. By staying informed and flexible, they navigated the turbulent waters, emerging stronger and wiser.

These examples highlight the importance of adaptability and the benefits of learning from those who've successfully navigated similar challenges. In a world where market conditions can change in the blink of an eye, having the ability to pivot and adjust your strategies is invaluable. It allows you to remain resilient, turning potential obstacles into opportunities. Cultivating this flexibility can enhance your trading experience, improving your chances of achieving your financial goals.

8.4 ENTRY AND EXIT QUIZ: TEST YOUR KNOWLEDGE

As you navigate the dynamic world of cryptocurrency trading, your ability to effectively identify entry and exit points can make a significant difference in your trading outcomes. It's time to put your newfound knowledge to the test with a quiz designed to reinforce key concepts and strategies discussed in the chapter. Consider each question carefully, drawing on the insights you've gathered so far.

True or False

1. Support and resistance levels can signal potential entry points by indicating where market trends might reverse. (True/False)
2. Trailing stop-loss orders remain fixed and do not move with the market. (True/False)
3. Selling during bullish exhaustion can help secure profits before a trend reverses. (True/False)
4. Perfectly timing each market move is essential for successful trading. (True/False)

Multiple Choice

5. Which tool is commonly used to identify potential entry points by analyzing price trends over time?
    - A) Bollinger Bands
    - B) Moving averages
    - C) On Balance Volume
6. When might a Fibonacci retracement level be beneficial in trading?
    - A) To determine the exact future price of an asset
    - B) To anticipate potential reversal levels based on previous price movements
    - C) To predict daily price changes
7. Which technical indicator might signal that an asset is overbought and it's time to consider exiting a trade?

  - A) On Balance Volume
  - B) Moving Average Convergence Divergence (MACD)
  - C) Relative Strength Index (RSI)
8. Which of the following can help traders refine their strategies in response to market changes?
  - A) Ignoring market sentiment
  - B) Backtesting strategies
  - C) Relying solely on gut feelings

Answers & Explanations

1. True
  - Explanation: Support and resistance levels are critical for identifying entry points based on market behavior.
2. False
  - Explanation: Trailing stop-loss orders adjust with market movements, helping protect profits dynamically.

3. True
  - Explanation: Recognizing bullish exhaustion signs can help traders lock in gains before the market shifts.
4. False
  - Explanation: Attempting to time the market perfectly is unrealistic and can lead to stress and poor decisions.
5. B) Moving averages
  - Explanation: Moving averages are crucial for spotting trends and potential reversals.
6. B) To anticipate potential reversal levels based on previous price movements
  - Explanation: Fibonacci retracement levels help traders spot areas where prices might bounce back.
7. C) Relative Strength Index (RSI)
  - Explanation: The RSI is a helpful tool for spotting overbought conditions.

3. B) Backtesting strategies
   - Explanation: Backtesting allows traders to test and refine their strategies using historical data.

Final Thoughts

This quiz is just a stepping stone on your path to becoming a more confident and informed trader. Understanding entry and exit strategies is pivotal, but it's just one part of the bigger picture in cryptocurrency trading. As you continue to engage with the material and apply these concepts, you'll find yourself better equipped to navigate the markets.

As we close this chapter, remember that trading is as much art as it is science. The skills you've learned here will serve you well as you move forward, but flexibility and ongoing learning are key. Next up is another critical component of your crypto journey: protecting your investments. Because no matter how skilled you become at reading charts or timing the market, none of it matters if your assets aren't secure.

CHAPTER 9
SECURITY AND SCAM PREVENTION

IMAGINE STEPPING into a bustling marketplace filled with traders, each promising the best deal you could ever imagine. The buzz and excitement are palpable, but so are the whispers of caution from seasoned traders – beware of the con artists in the crowd. In the world of cryptocurrency, identifying scams is like spotting a wolf in sheep's clothing. As you navigate this digital market, it's crucial to recognize the signs of deception that can lead to financial ruin.

9.1 IDENTIFYING COMMON CRYPTOCURRENCY SCAMS

Cryptocurrency scams are as varied as they are devious, preying on the unwary with promises that are too good to be true. Among the most infamous are **Ponzi schemes**, in which earlier investors are paid returns using funds from new participants rather than from actual profits. Closely related are **pyramid schemes**, which rely on constant recruitment to keep the money flowing. Both thrive on the illusion of profitability but inevitably collapse when new investment dries up. A well-known case was the BitConnect scam, which enticed users with the lure of guaranteed returns, only to unravel spectacularly, exposing the fraud and leaving countless victims in financial ruin.

Another prevalent scam is the **fake initial coin offering** (ICO), where scammers create a phony cryptocurrency or blockchain project to solicit investments. They often deploy slick marketing campaigns, complete with whitepapers and professional-looking websites, to lure unsuspecting investors. However, once they've collected enough funds, these scammers vanish, leaving behind a trail of broken promises and empty wallets. The initial excitement of getting in on the ground floor of the next big thing blinds many to the glaring lack of transparency and verifiable information, key red flags that something isn't quite right.

Phishing attacks represent another common threat, where scammers target your wallet credentials. These attacks often come in the form of emails or messages that appear to be from legitimate cryptocurrency exchanges or wallet providers. They trick you into revealing your private keys or login credentials, allowing them to gain access to your digital assets. The urgency in these messages, coupled with the use of official logos and branding, can easily fool even the cautious. But remember, no legitimate company will ever ask for your private keys or passwords. Always verify the sender and the website's authenticity before entering sensitive information.

The tactics used by scammers share common traits designed to deceive their victims. They promise guaranteed high returns, appealing to the greed in all of us. After all, who wouldn't want to double or triple their investment quickly? Yet, as the old saying goes, if it sounds too good to be true, it probably is. Scammers also employ urgency and pressure tactics, creating a false sense of FOMO or fear of missing out. This psychological manipulation exploits the human desire to seize opportunities before they're gone, pushing you to act quickly without thinking things through.

Another tactic is trust-building through fake testimonials or endorsements. You'll often see fabricated stories of people who supposedly struck it rich, complete with their photos and glowing reviews. This creates a sense of legitimacy and safety, lulling potential victims into a false sense of security. However, a quick reverse image search or a check of the social media profiles associated with these testimonials can often reveal their fraudulent nature. Genuine investment opportunities don't rely on such gimmicks to attract investors.

So, how do you protect yourself from these scams? The key lies in being vigilant and exercising due diligence. Before diving into any investment opportunity, conduct thorough research. Examine the project's whitepaper, scrutinize the team behind it, and look for third-party reviews and opinions. Check if the project is registered with relevant regulatory bodies; a lack of compliance is a major red flag. Legitimate projects will have nothing to hide and will openly share information about their operations, goals, and challenges.

9.2 SCAM PREVENTION STEPS

- **Research the Project**: Check the whitepaper, team credentials, and online presence.
- **Verify Regulatory Compliance**: Confirm registration with financial authorities.
- **Seek Third-Party Reviews**: Look for independent analysis and opinions.
- **Beware of High Returns Promises**: Question any guarantee of profits.
- **Check for Urgency Tactics**: Be cautious of time-limited offers and pressure to make an investment.
- **Investigate Testimonials**: Verify the authenticity of endorsements and success stories.

By staying informed and skeptical, you can navigate the cryptocurrency landscape with confidence. Remember, the digital world is filled with potential but also with pitfalls. Your best defense is knowledge, along with a healthy dose of skepticism.

9.3 STRENGTHENING SECURITY MEASURES FOR DIGITAL ASSETS

Imagine your digital assets as a treasure chest filled with valuables that could change your future. Just like you wouldn't leave such a chest unguarded, you shouldn't leave your cryptocurrency vulnerable to threats. The digital world is rife with risks, and without strong security practices, your assets are vulnerable. Preventing unauthorized access is crucial. Think of it like locking your front door before leaving home; it's a fundamental step in protecting what's yours. Yet, with digital currencies, simply locking the door isn't enough. You must also safeguard personal information, ensuring no one can impersonate you or gain access to your holdings. This is where robust security protocols come into play.

In the ever-evolving digital security landscape, advanced tools and techniques are your allies. **Multi-signature wallets** are a powerful option for added protection. They require multiple approvals before a transaction can be completed, much like needing two keys to open a safe. This means that even if one key is compromised, your assets remain secure. Meanwhile, **cold storage solutions** offer a secure storage option for long-term holdings. By keeping your assets offline, you shield them from online threats. It's like storing your treasures in a vault rather than a purse. **Hardware security modules** (HSMs) are hardware devices used to generate, store, and manage cryptographic keys securely. They provide an additional layer of defense and are an excellent choice for those who are serious about securing their digital wealth.

Regular security audits are an often overlooked but critical part of maintaining digital asset security. Imagine them as routine check-ups for your treasure chest, ensuring all locks and alarms are functioning properly. Conducting **personal security assessments** helps identify any weak spots in your defenses. It's like checking the windows and doors of your home to ensure they're locked tight. Engaging professional security firms can provide an added layer of scrutiny. These experts bring a wealth of knowledge and experience akin to hiring a security consultant to evaluate your home's defenses. Their insights can be invaluable in identifying vulnerabilities you might have missed.

To bolster your digital security, consider implementing a few key personal enhancements. **Enabling two-factor authentication** (2FA) is a straightforward yet effective step. It's like adding a second lock to your door, requiring both a password and a one-time code to gain access. **Regularly updating software and firmware** is another crucial measure. Just as you wouldn't ignore a recall notice for your car, you shouldn't disregard updates for your digital tools. These updates often include patches for known vulnerabilities, closing doors that hackers might exploit. Using **encrypted communication channels** (e.g., Signal, WhatsApp, or secure email) can further protect your information. It's like speaking in code that only you and your intended recipient understand, keeping your communications safe from prying eyes.

9.4 PERSONAL SECURITY ENHANCEMENT GUIDE

- **Enable Two-Factor Authentication (2FA)**: This requires a second form of verification and adds an extra layer of protection.
- **Regular Software Updates**: Keep all your software and firmware up to date to patch vulnerabilities.
- **Encrypted Communication Channels**: Use end-to-end encryption or secure email services to protect your communications.
- **Periodic Security Audits:** Regularly assess your security measures and address potential vulnerabilities.
- **Cold Storage Solutions**: Store long-term holdings offline to protect against online threats.
- **Multi-Signature Wallets**: Require multiple transaction approvals to add an additional layer of security.
- **Hardware Security Modules (HSMs)**: Use hardware-level security to protect digital assets.

In this digital age, your security measures must be as dynamic and adaptable as the threats you face. By implementing these strategies and regularly reviewing your defenses, you can safeguard your digital assets against the many challenges the cryptocurrency world presents.

9.5 REAL-LIFE SCAM EXAMPLES AND HOW TO AVOID THEM

Imagine the feeling of watching your hard-earned money vanish into thin air. This is the harsh reality that many investors faced during some of the most infamous cryptocurrency scams. These real-life examples serve as cautionary tales and as learning experiences for anyone venturing into the world of digital assets. One of the most notorious and devastating incidents in cryptocurrency history was the hack of the Mt. Gox exchange. At its peak, Mt. Gox was a giant in the crypto world, handling roughly 70% of all global Bitcoin transactions. For many early adopters, it was the primary gateway into cryptocurrency, trusted, widely used, and seen as the backbone of Bitcoin trading. However, that trust was catastrophically broken in 2014 when the exchange suffered a massive security breach. Approximately 850,000 Bitcoins – worth hundreds of millions of dollars at the time and exponentially more today – were stolen, vanishing without a trace.

The hack didn't just cripple the exchange; it sent shockwaves throughout the entire crypto community. It exposed serious flaws in the platform's security infrastructure, as well as a disturbing lack of internal oversight, transparency, and basic financial controls. For many users, the fallout was financially devastating – some lost their life savings or entire crypto portfolios overnight, with little to no recourse.

The Mt. Gox disaster became a wake-up call for the industry, underscoring the inherent risks of storing digital assets on centralized exchanges. It highlighted the importance of user education, robust cybersecurity protocols, and the need for better regulatory frameworks to protect investors. To this day, Mt. Gox serves as a cautionary tale – an enduring reminder that while the promise of cryptocurrency is revolutionary, it is not without its pitfalls.

Another alarming case was the OneCoin Ponzi scheme. Marketed as a revolutionary cryptocurrency, OneCoin claimed to be the next big thing, promising unparalleled returns. The reality, however, was far from these claims. It was a classic Ponzi scheme, where initial investors were paid with funds from new investors. With no actual blockchain or cryptocurrency to back its claims, OneCoin was all smoke and mirrors. The scheme's leaders, including Ruja Ignatova, who dubbed herself the "Cryptoqueen," exploited trust by leveraging fake authority and complex jargon to confuse and mislead thousands globally. The operation eventually collapsed, leading to arrests and ongoing legal battles. Victims were left grappling with not just financial ruin but also the emotional toll of being deceived by what they thought was a legitimate investment.

The BitConnect collapse is another stark reminder of the perils lurking in the cryptocurrency world. BitConnect promised guaranteed high returns through a lending program, where investors exchanged Bitcoin for BitConnect Coins (BCC). Promoters used flashy presentations and fake testimonials to lure in unsuspecting investors. But it was all a mirage. The platform operated as a Ponzi scheme, using new investments to pay returns to earlier investors, creating an illusion of profitability. When the scheme unraveled in 2018, the BCC value plummeted, and investors faced enormous losses. The fallout was immense, with legal actions against the founders and promoters, including charges of fraud and conspiracy.

These scams share common tactics that prey on trust and authority. Scammers often pose as industry experts or leverage the endorsement of celebrities to build credibility. They create complex layers of operation that seem legitimate from the outside but, upon closer inspection, reveal inconsistencies and a lack of transparency. This complexity is designed to confuse potential investors, making it difficult to discern the truth. As seen in these cases, the consequences for victims are devastating. The financial losses are just one aspect. Many face legal challenges as they try to recover their funds, while others deal with the emotional impact of being scammed. Trust, once broken, is hard to rebuild, and the stigma of being a victim can linger.

However, these stories are not just cautionary tales – they also provide valuable lessons. One of the most effective ways to avoid falling for scams is to approach every opportunity with a critical eye. When an opportunity seems too good to be true, it's worth taking a step back and scrutinizing the details. Start by doing your homework. Dig into the project's whitepaper, review its business model, and learn about the team behind it. Transparency is a key indicator of legitimacy – credible ventures are usually open about their structure, goals, and regulatory standing. Look for signs of compliance, such as registration with financial authorities and clear communication channels.

A helpful tip from the Federal Trade Commission (ftc.gov): before investing, run a quick online search using the name of the cryptocurrency, company, or founder paired with terms like "scam," "complaint," or "review." This simple step can uncover troubling patterns or user experiences that aren't immediately obvious. In the world of crypto, where innovation moves fast and regulation often lags behind, doing your due diligence is your best form of protection.

Learning from past mistakes also builds resilience. Understanding how these scams operate allows you to develop strategies to recognize red flags early on. This knowledge empowers you to make informed decisions, reducing the risk of falling victim to similar schemes. The cryptocurrency landscape is evolving, and being informed is your best defense against fraud. While the digital world offers exciting opportunities, navigating it with caution and awareness is crucial, as well as ensuring that your investments are secure and sound. As you move forward, keep these lessons in mind and use them to guide your decisions, protecting yourself from the pitfalls that have deceived many before you.

In the next chapter, we'll explore the importance of staying informed and connected within the cryptocurrency community, as knowledge and collaboration are key components to thriving in this dynamic environment.

CHAPTER 10
STAYING INFORMED AND CONNECTED

PICTURE THE CRYPTOCURRENCY market as a fast-paced race, where the track changes every few laps, and new competitors join in without warning. Staying informed isn't just about keeping pace; it's about anticipating those twists and turns before they happen. Whether you're a seasoned trader or just starting your crypto journey, understanding market trends and updates is vital. These insights help you make smarter trading decisions, spot emerging opportunities, and avoid potential pitfalls. The crypto world is dynamic, and keeping up with the latest developments can guide you in making timely and informed investment choices.

Tracking market trends means you're always a step ahead, ready to seize new opportunities before they become mainstream. When you anticipate market movements, you position yourself to make strategic decisions that align with your investment goals. For example, understanding when a particular cryptocurrency is gaining traction allows you to invest early, potentially maximizing your returns. Similarly, identifying when the market is cooling down gives you the chance to protect your investments by reallocating your assets or taking profits. By staying informed, you become a proactive participant in the market rather than a reactive observer, enhancing your ability to navigate the ever-changing crypto landscape.

To stay current, you need access to reliable and timely information. Thankfully, there are several platforms dedicated to providing the latest updates and trends in the crypto space. **CoinDesk** and **Cointelegraph** are two reputable news outlets that cover a wide range of topics, from major market moves to regulatory changes. These platforms provide in-depth analysis and expert opinions that help you understand the broader market context. Meanwhile, social media channels like **Twitter** and **Reddit** offer real-time updates and community discussions, where you can gauge market sentiment and learn from fellow investors. Market analysis blogs and newsletters, such as those from **Bankless**, focus on niche areas like decentralized finance (DeFi) and offer insights that might not make it to mainstream news.

However, the vast amount of information available can be overwhelming, making it crucial to filter out the noise. To do this, set up news alerts for specific cryptocurrencies you're interested in, ensuring you receive relevant updates without being bombarded by irrelevant information. Following reputable analysts and influencers who have a track record of accurate predictions can also provide you with valuable insights. These experts often share their analyses and forecasts, giving you a glimpse into potential market shifts. By focusing on reliable sources and experts, you can build a curated feed of information that enhances your understanding without overwhelming you.

Key market indicators act as signals to help you assess the current market climate and anticipate future trends. Monitoring trading volume fluctuations is essential, as sudden increases or decreases can signify shifts in investor interest or market sentiment. High trading volumes often indicate strong market activity, which can lead to price movements, while low volumes might suggest consolidation or a lack of interest. Sentiment analysis tools, which track social media mentions and news coverage, provide insights into how the market feels about specific cryptocurrencies. Positive sentiment often precedes price rallies, while negative sentiment can signal potential downturns. By monitoring these indicators, you can make informed decisions about when to enter or exit positions, optimizing your investment strategy.

Reflection Section: Staying Ahead

Take a moment to consider your current approach to staying

informed. Reflect on the sources you rely on and how effectively they serve your needs. Write down three trusted sources you plan to follow regularly and note any adjustments you might want to make to your information-gathering strategy. This exercise will help you refine your approach and remain connected to the most relevant and valuable insights in the crypto market.

10.1 JOINING CRYPTOCURRENCY COMMUNITIES FOR SUPPORT

Engaging with cryptocurrency communities offers an experience unlike any other. Imagine walking into a bustling room filled with people who share your interests, ready to exchange ideas, offer advice, and discuss market movements. These communities provide a space to connect with like-minded individuals who understand both the excitement and the challenges of navigating the crypto world. It's more than just networking; it's about finding your tribe. Whether you're seeking answers to complex questions or simply looking for encouragement, these communities are there to offer support and guidance. You become part of a collective journey where everyone is invested in learning and growing together.

Being part of these communities enables you to access a wealth of knowledge from diverse perspectives. Each member brings unique experiences and insights, enriching discussions and broadening your understanding of the market. This diversity is invaluable, as it helps you see issues from different angles and encourages you to think critically. Engaging with people with various expertise levels – from beginners to seasoned traders – allows you to learn new strategies and avoid potential pitfalls. It's like having a personal advisory board, ready to share insights and help you make informed decisions.

Reddit's **r/cryptocurrency** is one of the most popular forums for crypto enthusiasts. Here, you'll find vibrant discussions on everything from trading tips to regulatory updates. It's a place where you can ask questions and receive answers from experienced community members. The subreddit offers a mix of news, analysis, and personal stories that keep you informed and engaged. Similarly, **Telegram** and **Discord** groups have become essential for real-time communication and updates. These platforms host a variety of channels dedicated to specific cryptocurrencies, trading strategies, and market news. They provide a more interactive experience, where you can participate in live discussions and chats with other members.

In addition to r/cryptocurrency, there are many other subreddits that offer specialized information and support. Subreddits focused on specific coins, such as **r/Bitcoin** or **r/Ethereum**, offer targeted advice and discussions. They can be helpful if you're invested in or curious about particular cryptocurrencies. Each subreddit has its unique culture and guidelines, so taking the time to explore and find the ones that resonate with you is worthwhile. Engaging in these spaces not only expands your knowledge but also builds a sense of belonging as you interact with people who share common interests.

While these communities are incredibly valuable, it's important to approach them with an open mind and a critical eye. Not every piece of advice will apply to your situation, and evaluating the credibility of the information you receive is crucial. Engage actively, ask questions, and don't hesitate to share your own experiences. By contributing to these communities, you not only enhance your learning but also give back, helping others in their crypto exploration. This reciprocal relationship fosters a supportive environment where everyone benefits from shared knowledge and experiences.

10.2 TOOLS FOR MONITORING YOUR INVESTMENTS

Navigating the world of cryptocurrency can feel like you're in the middle of a bustling marketplace, with prices fluctuating and new opportunities emerging at every turn. Having the right tools is crucial to keep track of your investments and make informed decisions. Imagine having a personal assistant who monitors your assets while you focus on other important tasks. **Portfolio tracking apps** are designed to do just that. They help you manage your cryptocurrency investments by providing a real-time overview of your holdings, tracking performance, and offering insights that guide your investment strategies. These digital tools can be a game-changer, offering convenience and clarity in a fast-paced market.

One of the standout features of portfolio tracking apps is their comprehensive dashboard views. Picture a control center where you can see all your investments at a glance, from Bitcoin to the most obscure altcoin. This overview provides a snapshot of your current portfolio value and highlights changes in performance, helping you spot trends and make quick adjustments. Real-time price alerts are another key feature, sending notifications directly to your device whenever significant price movements occur. This allows you to react promptly to market changes, whether selling an asset at a peak or buying during a dip. Customizable alerts and notifications enhance this experience, letting you set specific criteria for alerts, such as price thresholds or percentage changes, ensuring you get the information that matters most to you.

Choosing the right investment tracking tool can seem overwhelming, given the many options available. However, focusing on a few key criteria can simplify the process. Start with the user interface and ease of use. A tool with an intuitive design will make navigation and data interpretation much simpler, reducing the learning curve. Integration with exchanges and wallets is another important factor. The ability to sync with the platforms you already use means you can import data seamlessly, minimizing manual entry and potential errors. Additionally, consider the range of features offered. Some tools provide basic tracking functions, while others offer advanced analytics, tax reporting, and integration with other asset classes, catering to diverse needs and preferences.

Among the popular investment tools, **Blockfolio** stands out for its robust portfolio management capabilities. It lets you track your investments across multiple exchanges, providing a holistic view of your holdings. **CoinGecko** is another favorite, especially for those who value detailed market data insights. It offers information on market trends, price movements, and even social media sentiment, giving you a well-rounded perspective on your assets. For those interested in advanced charting and technical analysis, **TradingView** offers a suite of features that cater to both beginners and seasoned traders, with customizable charts and a community of analysts sharing their insights. Each of these tools brings unique strengths to the table, and finding the one that aligns with your investment goals can significantly enhance your strategy.

Incorporating a portfolio tracker into your investment routine streamlines your management process and empowers you with the knowledge needed to make strategic decisions. It's like having a personal financial advisor who never sleeps, constantly analyzing data and trends to provide you with actionable insights. This level of oversight is particularly beneficial in the volatile world of cryptocurrency, where prices can change in the blink of an eye. By leveraging these tools, you can maintain a clear understanding of your portfolio's performance, identify improvement areas, and capitalize on opportunities as they arise, all while minimizing risks associated with market fluctuations.

10.3 CONTINUOUS LEARNING: RECOMMENDED RESOURCES

In the fast-paced world of cryptocurrency, staying informed is more than a good practice – it's a necessity. This ever-changing landscape requires constant adaptation to new technologies and a keen awareness of market trends. The crypto environment moves quickly, with innovations emerging almost daily. If you want to stay ahead, you must commit to continuous learning. This means not only keeping up with the latest advancements but also understanding how these changes impact your investments. Being proactive in your education helps you anticipate shifts, making you better equipped to respond to market dynamics. It's about being in the driver's seat, ready to navigate whatever comes your way.

To deepen your knowledge, it's important to tap into various educational resources that cater to different learning styles and preferences. Online courses and webinars offer structured learning, providing in-depth insights into specific topics. Websites like **edX** offer courses that cover everything from the basics of blockchain to advanced trading strategies. These courses are designed to fit into your schedule, allowing you to learn at your own pace. Meanwhile, **cryptocurrency books** and podcasts offer flexibility and depth, perfect for those who prefer to absorb information more leisurely. Books can be a great way to delve into the historical context and theoretical underpinnings of crypto, while **podcasts** often feature expert interviews and discussions on current trends, making them a great companion during a commute or workout.

Diverse resource types enrich your learning experience, ensuring you gain a well-rounded understanding of the crypto world. **Video tutorials**, for example, are perfect for visual learners who benefit from seeing concepts in action. Watching a step-by-step guide on setting up a wallet or using a trading platform can demystify processes that seem complex on paper. Similarly, **interviews with industry leaders** provide valuable perspectives and firsthand insights into the market's inner workings. Listening to how seasoned investors approach their strategies or how developers innovate within the blockchain space can inspire and inform your own practices.

Adopting effective learning strategies to maximize the educational resources available is helpful. Start by setting clear learning goals. Determine what you want to achieve, whether it's mastering technical analysis or understanding regulatory frameworks. Clear goals guide your focus and keep you motivated. Schedule regular study sessions, carving out dedicated time in your week to engage with learning materials. Consistency is key, as regular engagement helps reinforce new knowledge and build expertise over time. It's also important to stay curious and open-minded, willing to explore new topics and challenge existing assumptions.

Taking notes is another effective way to enhance your learning. Writing down key points reinforces what you've learned and serves as a handy reference for future review. Create a personal glossary of terms and concepts as you encounter them, ensuring you understand the language of crypto. Engaging in discussions with peers can further solidify your understanding, as teaching others is a powerful way to deepen your own comprehension. By sharing insights and asking questions, you also benefit from the collective knowledge of your peers, gaining new perspectives and clarifying uncertainties.

As you immerse yourself in continuous learning, remember that the goal is to accumulate information and apply it effectively. The cryptocurrency world is vast, and there's always more to discover.

Embrace the journey of learning as a lifelong endeavor, one that empowers you to navigate the market with confidence and resilience. With a commitment to education and a willingness to adapt, you position yourself for success in the ever-evolving realm of cryptocurrency. As you build your knowledge and skills, you'll find yourself better prepared to seize opportunities and tackle challenges, paving the way for a rewarding experience in the world of digital assets. In the next chapter, we'll explore the legal and tax considerations critical for safeguarding your investments and ensuring compliance. Stay curious, stay informed, and keep honing your skills.

CHAPTER 11
NAVIGATING LEGAL AND TAX CONSIDERATIONS

NAVIGATING cryptocurrency regulations is like driving on a busy highway with many lanes and exit ramps leading to different destinations. In this complex network, understanding the legal landscape is your GPS – providing direction, avoiding wrong turns, and helping you stay on the right path. As a budding cryptocurrency investor, you must know the rules and regulations governing this dynamic space.

They vary significantly from country to country and can impact how you trade, invest, and even hold cryptocurrencies. Let's take a closer look at why knowing these regulations is so crucial.

Regulations around cryptocurrency are as diverse as the countries from which they originate. Some regions roll out the red carpet for digital currencies, creating a crypto-friendly environment that fosters innovation and growth. Others, however, are more restrictive, placing tight controls on what can and cannot be done. This diversity means that where you live can significantly affect your cryptocurrency activities. Understanding the local laws is crucial, not only to stay compliant but also to make informed decisions. If you're trading in a country with stringent regulations, you might face more challenges than in a jurisdiction that embraces digital currencies.

Regulatory bodies play a pivotal role in shaping the cryptocurrency landscape. In the United States, the Securities and Exchange Commission (SEC) plays a central role in regulating crypto-related securities, aiming to protect investors and ensure fair, transparent markets. Across the Atlantic, the UK's Financial Conduct Authority (FCA) oversees digital asset activities, ensuring companies operate legally while prioritizing consumer protection. In Japan, the Financial Services Agency (FSA) regulates cryptocurrency exchanges, promoting stability and transparency in the market. Each of these bodies brings unique perspectives and policies, affecting how cryptocurrencies are managed and traded. Their roles are integral to maintaining trust and order within the crypto world.

Keeping up with regulatory changes is like staying updated with weather forecasts when planning a trip – conditions can shift rapidly, and failing to prepare can lead to trouble. Recent developments have shown just how quickly the regulatory landscape can shift. The European Union recently finalized the Markets in Crypto-Assets (MiCA) regulation to provide clarity and consistency across member states. In the United States, a cohesive regulatory framework for digital assets is slowly emerging, though its final shape is still uncertain. Meanwhile, China has cracked down on crypto mining activities, sending shockwaves through the global mining community. Such developments underscore the importance of staying informed about regulatory updates, as they can have far-reaching implications for your investments and strategies.

These developments demonstrate how regulatory actions can significantly impact the market. China's ban on Initial Coin Offerings (ICOs), for example, disrupted how projects raise funds. On the other hand, El Salvador's bold move to adopt Bitcoin as legal tender illustrates how regulation can propel cryptocurrencies into mainstream use. Each of these cases reflects the powerful influence that government decisions can exert on investor behavior, innovation, and market dynamics. As a crypto enthusiast, being abreast of these changes helps you navigate the market with agility and foresight.

Staying compliant with regulations is not just about avoiding legal troubles; it's about building a sustainable and ethical approach to investing. Regularly check official regulatory websites for updates and engage with compliance-focused news outlets to stay informed. This proactive approach ensures that you're continually operating within the bounds of the law, safeguarding both your investments and your peace of mind. In the ever-evolving world of cryptocurrency, knowledge is your most powerful ally. By understanding and respecting the rules of the road, you can steer clear of potential pitfalls and chart a course toward success. Refer to the section at the end of the chapter for a detailed listing of regulatory authorities in various countries.

11.1 TAX IMPLICATIONS OF CRYPTO: WHAT YOU NEED TO KNOW

Navigating the world of cryptocurrency taxes can feel like trying to find your way in a maze, but once you get the hang of it, the path becomes more apparent. Depending on where you live, cryptocurrencies might be taxed differently, and understanding these differences is crucial. In many countries, cryptocurrencies are treated as capital assets, much like stocks or real estate. This means that when you sell your crypto, your profit is subject to capital gains tax. This tax applies if your crypto's value has increased from when you bought it to when you sold it. However, not all crypto transactions are straightforward. For instance, trades between different cryptocurrencies can also trigger tax events, even if you haven't cashed out to traditional currency. In these cases, the tax authorities consider the trade as if you sold one asset and bought another, which can complicate things.

Taxable events in the crypto world are those moments when you might owe taxes. Selling your cryptocurrency for fiat currency, like dollars or euros, is the most common taxable event. But it's not the only one. Using your crypto to buy goods or services is also a taxable event. Think of it like this: if you buy a coffee with Bitcoin, you're effectively selling a portion of your Bitcoin, and any gain since you acquired that portion is taxable. Receiving cryptocurrency as payment or mining rewards is another scenario that triggers a tax obligation. In these cases, the crypto you receive is considered income, and you owe taxes based on its fair market value when you receive it. Each of these activities comes with its own rules, and understanding them is key to staying on the right side of the law.

Cryptocurrency taxation isn't without its challenges. One of the biggest hurdles is tracking the cost basis of your crypto assets, especially if you've made multiple transactions over time. The cost basis is the original value of your crypto when you acquired it, and it's used to calculate your capital gains or losses. Keeping accurate records can become a daunting task if you're buying and selling frequently. Furthermore, reporting requirements for small transactions can be just as rigorous as for larger ones, adding to the complexity. The lack of consistent global standards means that what works in one country might not apply in another, making cross-border crypto activities especially tricky. These challenges can make tax season a stressful time for crypto investors, but there are ways to ease the burden.

Fortunately, resources are available to help you navigate the complexities of crypto taxes. Platforms like Koinly and CryptoTrader.Tax are designed to assist with tracking your transactions and calculating your tax obligations. These tools can integrate with your exchanges and wallets, automatically pulling in your transaction data and simplifying the process. They offer a way to transform a potentially overwhelming task into something more manageable. For official guidelines, your best bet is to visit government tax websites. They provide up-to-date information on local tax laws and requirements, helping to ensure that you're in compliance with current regulations.

You can gain clarity and confidence in handling your crypto taxes by leveraging these resources. Refer to the section at the end of the chapter for a detailed listing of taxing authorities in various countries.

11.2 TRACKING TRANSACTIONS FOR TAX PURPOSES

Imagine you're assembling a puzzle. Each piece must fit perfectly to reveal the whole picture. In the world of cryptocurrency, accurate transaction tracking is that puzzle, crucial for clearly seeing your financial landscape and ensuring compliance with tax requirements. Keeping meticulous records of every crypto transaction is like laying down those puzzle pieces one by one. Each record serves as proof of purchase and sale, painting a detailed picture of your crypto dealings. This precision becomes vital when calculating capital gains and losses, which are often based on the difference between your purchase and sale prices. Without these records, you could find yourself struggling to determine your tax obligations accurately, potentially leading to costly mistakes or penalties.

To maintain accuracy, consider a few practical tips for tracking your cryptocurrency transactions. Start by keeping detailed logs of every buy and sell date and the corresponding prices. This might seem tedious, but it is a solid foundation for calculating your gains or losses. You can jot these down in a dedicated notebook or a digital document, whichever is more convenient for you. When recording a trade, you should track the following information:

- Date and time of trade
- Asset traded
- Amount bought/sold
- Price (in USD or local currency)
- Transactions fees
- Exchange/platform used

Integrating your records with exchanges and wallets enhances your ability to track transactions seamlessly. Many exchanges offer downloadable transaction histories, allowing you to import data directly into your tracking system. This integration can save time and reduce the likelihood of errors, ensuring that all your records are comprehensive and up-to-date.

There are several tools and techniques at your disposal for tracking your cryptocurrency transactions. For those who prefer a hands-on approach, spreadsheet templates offer a straightforward way to track your transactions manually. With some customization, you can create a personalized system that fits your needs, helping you stay organized and focused. However, if manual tracking doesn't suit you, portfolio tracking software like CoinTracking might be the solution. Tracking platforms automate much of the process, pulling data from various exchanges and wallets to provide a comprehensive overview of your crypto activities. They offer features like real-time tracking, tax reporting, and performance analysis, making them an invaluable asset for any crypto enthusiast.

Those looking to take automation to the next level should consider using tools like CryptoTrader.Tax. This software specializes in tax calculations, taking the guesswork out of determining your tax liabilities. By inputting your transaction data, you can generate detailed tax reports that outline your gains, losses, and other relevant information. This level of automation simplifies the process and provides peace of mind, knowing that your calculations are accurate and compliant with tax regulations. With these tools, you can streamline your tracking efforts, allowing you to focus more on your investment strategies and less on administrative tasks.

11.3 LEGAL AND TAX RESOURCES

Navigating cryptocurrency's legal and tax landscape isn't just about following rules; it's about making informed decisions that protect your investments and ensure long-term success. Reliable information sources are your best ally in this endeavor. Government websites are a goldmine for the latest updates on regulations and tax obligations. These sites often provide official guidelines and answers to frequently asked questions, which can help clear up any uncertainties you may have. Regulatory websites offer insights into the latest legal developments, keeping you informed about changes that could impact your cryptocurrency activities. For a broader perspective, turn to compliance-focused news outlets and industry publications. These sources offer in-depth analyses, expert opinions, and detailed reports on trends, providing a well-rounded view of the crypto landscape. Subscribing to newsletters from trusted organizations can also keep you in the loop, delivering essential information straight to your inbox.

Participating in professional networks is another way to stay ahead in the crypto world. Joining groups and associations that focus on cryptocurrency law and taxation gives you access to a wealth of knowledge and experience. These communities often host discussions, share resources, and provide valuable insights from professionals who navigate the legal and tax terrain daily. Online forums for tax professionals can be particularly beneficial, allowing you to pose questions, exchange ideas, and learn from others' experiences. Engaging with these networks enhances your understanding and connects you with like-minded individuals who can offer support and guidance when needed.

Continuous learning is key to thriving in the ever-evolving crypto environment. Webinars and online courses focused on the legal and tax aspects of cryptocurrency are excellent resources for expanding your knowledge. These educational opportunities are often led by experts who delve into complex topics, breaking them down into digestible pieces. Workshops by legal professionals provide hands-on learning experiences, enabling you to apply what you've learned in practical scenarios. Online courses on crypto tax compliance can equip you with the skills needed to handle your tax obligations confidently. The more you learn, the better equipped you'll be to make informed decisions that benefit your crypto investments.

Keeping an eye on legislative developments is crucial for staying informed about potential legal changes that could affect your cryptocurrency activities. Tracking legislative proposals allows you to anticipate shifts in the regulatory landscape, giving you time to adjust your strategies accordingly. Advocacy groups play a significant role in shaping legislation, and engaging with them can provide insights into the direction of future regulations. These groups often work to protect the interests of crypto investors, advocating for fair and balanced policies. By staying engaged and informed, you can confidently navigate the complex legal environment, ensuring that your investments remain secure and compliant.

11.4 NEW U.S. CRYPTO TAX RULES

In 2024, the IRS rolled out several new rules to improve how cryptocurrency and other digital assets are taxed and reported. One significant change was the introduction of new reporting requirements for brokers, including crypto exchanges, wallet providers, and some payment apps. These platforms are now required to report customer transactions to the IRS, similar to how stock brokers report trades. To make this process easier, the IRS created a new form called **Form 1099-DA**, which brokers will begin using in 2025 to report the amount you sold crypto for. Starting in 2026, the form will also include how much you originally paid (your cost basis), making it easier for both you and the IRS to calculate your gains or losses.

There's also a law in progress called the FIT21 Act (short for "Financial Innovation and Technology for the 21st Century Act"). While not yet law, this bill aims to bring clarity to how digital assets are regulated. It will split oversight between the SEC (Securities and Exchange Commission) and the CFTC (Commodity Futures Trading Commission), helping to define which assets are treated as securities and which are commodities. The goal is to support innovation in the crypto space while establishing clear, consistent rules.

As cryptocurrency laws continue to evolve, staying informed is more important than ever to remain compliant and avoid surprises come tax season. Monitor changes using the resources outlined in this chapter and consult your tax professional for guidance specific to your circumstances.

11.5 REAL-LIFE TAX SCENARIOS: LESSONS LEARNED

Let's dive into some real-life tax scenarios that cryptocurrency investors have faced. These stories offer valuable lessons and insights into navigating the often complicated world of crypto taxes. One common situation involves reporting errors, where investors might have inadvertently made mistakes in their filings. These errors can lead to audits, which are stressful and can result in penalties. For example, an investor might have misreported the cost basis of their crypto assets, leading to incorrect capital gains calculations. When the tax authorities notice discrepancies, they may launch an audit to investigate the issue. This process can be time-consuming and requires the investor to provide documentation to support their claims. Mistakes like these highlight the importance of accuracy and the potential consequences of oversight.

Another scenario emphasizes the benefits of early tax planning. Imagine an investor who meticulously plans their crypto transactions throughout the year. By keeping detailed records and consulting with tax professionals, they can strategically manage their holdings to minimize tax liabilities. For instance, they may engage in **tax-loss harvesting**, selling underperforming assets at a loss to offset capital gains elsewhere in their portfolio. This proactive approach allows them to reduce their overall tax bill and optimize their investment strategy. Planning and implementing strategies like tax-loss harvesting can significantly impact an investor's bottom line, highlighting the importance of planning and intelligent money management.

Challenges often arise when handling discrepancies in transaction records. This can be particularly problematic for investors who frequently trade or use multiple exchanges. Discrepancies might occur when the recorded transaction dates or amounts don't match the actual trades. Resolving such issues requires carefully reviewing all records, often comparing exchange histories with personal logs. This can be tedious but is necessary to ensure accuracy. When errors are found, amending incorrect filings becomes crucial. Investors must file amended tax returns, providing corrected information and supporting documentation. Doing so promptly can help mitigate penalties and demonstrate a commitment to compliance.

The key takeaway from these experiences is the importance of keeping accurate records and filing your taxes on time, which avoids late fees and allows investors to address any discrepancies before they escalate. Additionally, leveraging tax-loss harvesting as a strategy can turn losses into opportunities, providing a way to balance gains and reduce taxable income. These lessons underscore the value of being proactive in managing cryptocurrency taxes. Regular consultations with tax professionals can offer guidance tailored to an individual's unique situation, providing clarity and confidence in their tax strategies.

Tax regulations constantly evolve, and staying informed ensures that investors remain compliant and take advantage of new opportunities. This proactive approach can prevent surprises and allow for strategic adjustments in response to changes in the tax landscape. By adopting a proactive mindset and leveraging available resources, investors can navigate the complexities of crypto taxes with greater ease and success.

11.6 REGULATORY AND TAX RESOURCES

Here's a list of key cryptocurrency regulators and tax authorities in several major countries. This includes financial regulators (who oversee crypto markets and exchanges) and tax authorities (who enforce crypto taxation and reporting).

Note: This list is not exhaustive and may change as regulations and oversight continue to evolve. It's crucial to identify the relevant regulators and tax authorities in your own country or region and stay informed as policies develop.

United States

- **Financial Regulators:**
  - **SEC** (Securities and Exchange Commission) – Regulates crypto as securities (e.g., ICOs, investment contracts).
  - **CFTC** (Commodity Futures Trading Commission) – Treats crypto as commodities; oversees derivatives and futures.
  - **FinCEN** (Financial Crimes Enforcement Network) – Enforces AML/KYC rules and monitors illicit activity.

  - **OCC** (Office of the Comptroller of the Currency) – Oversees national banks offering crypto services.

- **Tax Authority:**
  - **IRS** (Internal Revenue Service) – Treats crypto as property; requires capital gains reporting.

European Union

- **Financial Regulators:**
  - **ESMA** (European Securities and Markets Authority) – Provides oversight and coordination among member states.
  - **ECB** (European Central Bank) – Monitors crypto implications for monetary policy and financial stability.
  - **MiCA** (Markets in Crypto-Assets Regulation) – New EU-wide regulatory framework for crypto service providers (phased in from 2024–2025).

- **Tax Authorities:**
  - Varies by member country; common guidance:
    - Crypto is typically taxed as capital gains.
    - Examples:
      - Germany – Federal Central Tax Office (BZSt)
      - France – Direction Générale des Finances Publiques (DGFiP)
      - Netherlands – Belastingdienst

China

- **Financial Regulators:**
  - **PBoC** (People's Bank of China) – Enforces bans on crypto trading and mining; promotes digital yuan – Central Bank Digital Currency (CBDC).
  - **CAC** (Cyberspace Administration of China) – Regulates blockchain-related services.

- **Tax Authority:**
  - **SAT** (State Administration of Taxation) – While crypto trading is banned, ownership may still have tax implications under certain conditions.

Japan

- **Financial Regulators:**
  - **FSA** (Financial Services Agency) – Licenses and regulates crypto exchanges; enforces strict AML/KYC.

- **Tax Authority:**
  - **NTA** (National Tax Agency) – Treats crypto as "miscellaneous income" for individuals; subject to progressive income tax.

United Kingdom

- **Financial Regulators:**
  - **FCA** (Financial Conduct Authority) – Regulates crypto firms, especially in areas of AML and advertising.

- **Tax Authority:**
  - **HMRC** (Her Majesty's Revenue and Customs) – Treats crypto as property; capital gains tax applies to trading and investing.

Canada

- **Financial Regulators:**
  - **CSA** (Canadian Securities Administrators) – Coordinates provincial securities laws; crypto is treated as securities in many cases.
  - **FINTRAC** (Financial Transactions and Reports Analysis Centre) – AML/KYC compliance for crypto businesses.

- **Tax Authority:**
  - **CRA** (Canada Revenue Agency) – Taxes crypto as capital gains or business income, depending on activity.

CONCLUSION

Congratulations! You've made it to the end of our journey together, exploring the exciting and sometimes daunting world of cryptocurrency. We've covered a lot of ground, from understanding the basics of blockchain technology to developing personalized trading strategies and navigating the legal and tax implications of your investments. It's been an incredible adventure, and you should be proud of the progress you've made.

As we wrap up, I want to emphasize the importance of building a strong foundation in cryptocurrency. Understanding key concepts like wallets, exchanges, and market analysis is crucial to your success as an investor. These fundamentals will serve as your anchor, providing stability and confidence as you navigate the crypto landscape.

Remember, the world of cryptocurrency is constantly evolving, with new technologies, trends, and opportunities emerging daily. To stay ahead of the curve, embracing continuous learning is essential. Keep exploring, researching, and staying informed about the latest developments in the space. The resources and strategies discussed throughout this book will be invaluable in your ongoing education.

As you continue your crypto journey, don't forget the importance of risk management. Diversifying your portfolio, controlling your emotions, and using tools like stop-loss orders can help you weather the market's ups and downs. These strategies will be your lifeline, protecting your investments and helping you make informed decisions in the face of volatility.

One of the most powerful aspects of the cryptocurrency community is the sense of camaraderie and support. Engaging with others who share your passion for crypto can be incredibly rewarding. Join forums, attend meetups, and participate in online discussions. You'll find a wealth of knowledge, inspiration, and friendship among your fellow enthusiasts.

So, what are the key takeaways from our time together? First and foremost, set clear investment goals and develop a personalized trading plan. Understand the importance of market analysis, both technical and fundamental. Learn to identify and avoid scams, and always prioritize the security of your digital assets. These insights will be your guiding light as you navigate the crypto space.

With the knowledge and tools you've gained from this book, you can confidently engage in cryptocurrency trading and investment. But don't just take my word for it – put your skills into practice! Set up a wallet, join a community, and start trading with a small investment. The best way to learn is by doing, and every experience, whether a success or a setback, will be a valuable lesson.

As you embark on this exciting new chapter, remember that your learning journey is never truly over. Keep exploring, keep asking questions, and keep pushing yourself to grow. The cryptocurrency world is full of possibilities, and with dedication and perseverance, you can achieve your financial goals.

I'll leave you with this final thought: you have the power to shape your financial future. The cryptocurrency market may be unpredictable, but with the proper knowledge, mindset, and support, you can navigate it with confidence. Embrace the opportunities, learn from the challenges, and never stop believing in yourself. Now go forth and seize the incredible opportunities that await you in the world of cryptocurrency. The future is yours for the taking!

REFERENCES

- "Crypto Losses" by Jeffrey A. Maine and Xuan-Thao Nguyen. (2025). Retrieved from https://digitalcommons.mainelaw.maine.edu/faculty-publications/163/
- 10 Best Crypto Portfolio Trackers for Every Investor. (2025). Retrieved from https://coinbureau.com/analysis/best-crypto-portfolio-trackers/
- 11 Best Crypto Wallets of February 2025. (2025). Retrieved from https://money.com/best-crypto-wallets/
- 6 Best crypto paper trading apps & simulators in 2023. (2025). Retrieved from https://blog.tradingleagues.app/6-best-crypto-paper-trading-apps-simulators-in-2023/
- 8 Ways to Diversify Your Crypto Portfolio and Limit Risk. (2025). Retrieved from https://money.usnews.com/investing/cryptocurrency/articles/ways-to-diversify-your-crypto-portfolio-and-limit-risk
- Adaptability and Flexibility in Trading: Strategies for Success. (2025). Retrieved from https://www.quantifiedstrategies.com/adaptability-and-flexibility-in-trading/
- Avoid Fake Cryptocurrency Exchanges with This List. (2025). Retrieved from https://www.datavisor.com/wiki/fake-cryptocurrency-exchanges/
- Best Online Cryptocurrency Courses and Programs. (2025). Retrieved from https://www.edx.org/learn/cryptocurrency
- Blockchain - Wikipedia. (2025). Retrieved from https://en.wikipedia.org/wiki/Blockchain#:~:text=A%20blockchain%20was%20created%20by,Scott%20Stornetta%2C%20and%20Dave%20Bayer.
- Breaking news headlines: Impact on trading activity in the .... (2025). Retrieved from https://www.sciencedirect.com/science/article/abs/pii/S0264999323002092
- Case Studies: Successful Crypto Investments Backed by .... (2025). Retrieved from https://medium.com/@shuumar48/case-studies-successful-crypto-investments-backed-by-market-research-c9e431617ff5
- Case study - BitConnect cryptocurrency fraud. (2025). Retrieved from https://www.bdo.ca/insights/cryptocurrency-execs-charged-for-2-4-billion-ponzi-scheme
- Centralized vs. decentralized crypto exchanges. (2025). Retrieved from https://cointelegraph.com/learn/articles/centralized-vs-decentralized-crypto-exchanges
- Crypto technical indicators: A beginners guide | Kraken. (2025). Retrieved from https://www.kraken.com/learn/crypto-technical-indicators#:~:text=Common%20indicators%20include%20moving%20averages,OBV)%20for%20assessing%20directional%20volume.

REFERENCES

- Cryptocurrency Investment: Diversification or Risk?. (2025). Retrieved from https://rankiapro.com/en/insights/cryptocurrency-investment-diversification-risk/
- Day Trading vs. Swing Trading: What's the Difference?. (2025). Retrieved from https://www.investopedia.com/articles/active-trading/052815/pros-cons-day-trading-vs-swing-trading.asp
- Digital assets | Internal Revenue Service. (2025). Retrieved from https://www.irs.gov/filing/digital-assets
- Emotional trading in the cryptocurrency market. (2025). Retrieved from https://www.sciencedirect.com/science/article/abs/pii/S1544612320317268
- FBI Publishes 2023 Cryptocurrency Fraud Report. (2025). Retrieved from https://www.fbi.gov/news/press-releases/fbi-publishes-2023-cryptocurrency-fraud-report
- Global Crypto Regulation Report 2023. (2025). Retrieved from https://www.pwc.com/gx/en/about/new-ventures/global-crypto-regulation-report-2023.html
- Guide to Cryptocurrency Security. (2025). Retrieved from https://www.arkoselabs.com/explained/guide-to-cryptocurrency-security/
- How Does Cryptocurrency Work? A Beginner's Guide. (2025). Retrieved from https://www.coursera.org/articles/how-does-cryptocurrency-work
- How To Use Bollinger Bands In Crypto Trading | Mudrex Learn. (2025). Retrieved from https://mudrex.com/learn/bollinger-bands-in-crypto-trading/#:~:text=Bollinger%20Bands%20can%20be%20combined,into%20trend%20direction%20and%20momentum.
- How to Set up a Hardware Wallet: Step by step. (2025). Retrieved from https://materialbitcoin.com/en/blog/set-up-hardware-wallet/?srsltid=AfmBOopKtynwFYqIom1OlkKLPqDgrPU29XpW78eSxnaG-QXmX1xOsePn
- How to track cryptocurrency transactions: A complete guide. (2025). Retrieved from https://www.cointracker.io/blog/how-to-track-crypto-transactions
- Inside The Minds Of Top Crypto Traders: Success Stories & .... (2025). Retrieved from https://pi42.com/blog/inside-the-minds-of-top-crypto-traders/
- Introduction to smart contracts. (2025). Retrieved from https://ethereum.org/en/developers/docs/smart-contracts/
- KYC for crypto: Ensuring crypto security and compliance | Plaid. (2025). Retrieved from https://plaid.com/resources/compliance/kyc-crypto/#:~:text=What%20is%20KYC%20in%20cryptocurrency,other%20illegal%20or%20illicit%20activities.
- Nailing Your Crypto Goals. (2025). Retrieved from https://collectiveshift.io/beginner/planning-your-crypto-goals/
- Securing your wallet - Bitcoin. (2025). Retrieved from https://bitcoin.org/en/secure-your-wallet
- Stablecoins as a tool to mitigate the downside risk of .... (2025). Retrieved

from https://www.sciencedirect.com/science/article/pii/S1062940822001735

- Stop-Loss and Take-Profit Orders. (2025). Retrieved from https://help.crypto.com/en/articles/4453247-stop-loss-and-take-profit-orders
- The 20 Best Crypto News Websites in 2023. (2025). Retrieved from https://www.yadaontheblock.com/post/best-crypto-news-websites
- The Benefits of Diversification in Crypto. (2025). Retrieved from https://www.globalxetfs.com/the-benefits-of-diversification-in-crypto/
- Timing the Market: Myths and Realities for Crypto Investors. (2025). Retrieved from https://thesecretsandbox.com/2025/02/04/timing-the-market-myths-and-realities-for-crypto-investors/
- Top 12 Crypto Discord Servers to Join in 2025. (2025). Retrieved from https://dailycoin.com/top-10-crypto-discord-servers-to-join/
- Top Cryptocurrency Exchanges Ranked By Volume. (2025). Retrieved from https://coinmarketcap.com/rankings/exchanges/
- Top Cryptocurrency Myths. (2025). Retrieved from https://www.investopedia.com/tech/top-bitcoin-myths/
- Understanding Basic Candlestick Charts. (2025). Retrieved from https://www.investopedia.com/trading/candlestick-charting-what-is-it/
- Wallet troubleshooting and tips. (2025). Retrieved from https://help.coinbase.com/en/wallet/other-topics/troubleshooting-and-tips
- What Are the Legal Risks to Cryptocurrency Investors?. (2025). Retrieved from https://www.investopedia.com/tech/what-are-legal-risks-cryptocurrency-investors/
- What is Risk Tolerance in Crypto Trading - Altrady. (2025). Retrieved from https://www.altrady.com/crypto-trading/risk-management/risk-tolerance-crypto-trading#:~:text=To%20determine%20your%20risk%20tolerance,emotional%20capacity%20to%20handle%20losses.

www.ingramcontent.com/pod-product-compliance
Lightning Source LLC
LaVergne TN
LVHW022100200926
848481LV00003B/1004